Published in the United States by Beginnings.

ISBN-13: 978-0615569437
ISBN-10: 0615569439

Quotes from *Please Understand Me II*: *Temperament Character Intelligence* by David Keirsey used by permission from the author.

Manufactured in the U.S.A.
First edition published 2011.
Cover design by Stephanie Ann Adams, with thanks to Amy K. Harris and Tim Adams.

THE BEGINNING COUNSELOR'S SURVIVAL GUIDE:

THE NEW COUNSELOR'S PLAN FOR SUCCESS FROM PRACTICUM TO LICENSURE

By

Stephanie Ann Adams, MA

and

Carol R. Doss, PhD

MORE ADVANCE PRAISE FOR THE BEGINNING COUNSELOR'S SURVIVAL GUIDE

When I sat down to read Stephanie Adams and Carol Doss' new book, The Beginning Counselor's Survival Guide, I expected to see mostly old information re-hashed and re-packaged. But, I was wrong. Instead it is filled with practical, no-nonsense advice that every new mental health professional needs before they ever leave the halls of academia.

Adams' seems like a counselor's best friend, chatty and personable, as she guides new professionals through everything from how to choose a practicum site and supervisor to necessary steps for obtaining a license and beginning marketing. The seasoned contributions from Doss, like little whispers from a mentor who has your back, add gentle reminders and weight that every new professional needs to stay grounded and focused through this confusing and stressful journey.

This is the one book that every new mental health professional should pick up as soon as they enter graduate school. The Beginning Counselor's Survival Guide is a road map, a friend, and a security blanket all rolled into one. It's a book I wish I had had and one I will pass along to others needing to navigate the path to licensure and beyond.

Tamara Suttle, M.Ed., LPC

Also by Dr. Carol Doss

*Should I Leave Him? How to decide whether to move forward together –
or move on without him.* Adams Media, 2010. ISBN 978-1598699692

ACKNOWLEDGEMENTS

Stephanie would like to thank:

My husband, Tim, for supporting me and believing in my writing dreams. My parents, Andy and Patti Smith, for encouraging me from birth, educating me, and for thinking that everything I do is interesting and brilliant. My brothers, Sam, Shawn and Scott, for creating in me the desire to be someone they can look up to. The Smith family, the Adams family and the rest of my amazing in-laws for prayer and love. Diana Pitaru and all the members of The Counselors and Psychotherapists Network of North Texas, for their support and friendship. All the generous people that selflessly gave their time to help me edit the book: Sue Jamison, Leonard Stevens, K. Hill and Patti Smith. Tamara Suttle and David P. Diana, for reviewing the book and sharing their feedback. Dr. Roger Doss and Debbie Lee, for welcoming me into the Family Counseling Center, befriending me, and teaching me. And of course my writing partner Dr. Carol Doss, for being an amazing clinical supervisor, the voice of wisdom, and a perfect example of work-life balance. I still want to be like you when I grow up!

Carol would like to thank:

All the interns who've shared their growth with me.

From the both of us, thanks to:

David Keirsey and the Prometheus Nemesis Book Company for permission to use quotes and information from the book *Please Understand Me II: Temperament, Character, Intelligence* and Naomi Quenk and John Wiley & Sons for permission to quote the book *Essentials of Myers-Briggs Type Indicator Assessment.*

DEDICATION

We would like to dedicate this book to beginning counselors everywhere.
May you find your path and enjoy your journey.

INTRODUCTION

Why this book?

Honestly, I can't believe I get to be the first to write it. In my opinion, the need for this book has been a long time coming.

Potential counselors enter the field eager, motivated and excited. Unfortunately, by the time they leave their internship (if they are even lucky enough to get there) they are more often than not disillusioned, indebted and discouraged.

Why has this been acceptable for so long? In my mind, it's not. After all, we are the group of people responsible for the mental health and wellbeing of others. If we're not healthy, we're transmitting that unhealthiness to our clients, our co-workers, and our families. Emotional health is catching – as is emotional dysfunction. So why aren't we doing all we can to increase counselor support?

And why are we instead creating a culture of failure?

I can't count how many times I've heard:

"Clients will drain you dry."
"You can't make any money in this business."
"You're going to end up hating people in this job."

Well, that's encouraging, isn't it?

It's also – excuse me – absolute B.S. It doesn't have to be this way. I know very many healthy, happy, and well-adjusted counselors.

But the reason that those counselors became that way was hard work, self-care, and determination. Not because that was how they were trained in the beginning. Our schools teach us theories and research but not, as a matter of course, how to be healthy counselors. Why not? There could be any number of reasons. Some professors have been in academia so long they have lost the real-world experience with counseling. Other professors, those that do have knowledge and the desire to share, are not supported by grad school curricula in passing along these valuable insights to students. I do not believe it is a case of any individual professor's rebellion or lack of feeling. It is simply that a reliable, effective method for supporting new counselors is not built into the system. And as a result, it is not valued.

The reason I love the Beginning Counselor movement (the unofficial name for the collection of wonderful new counselors at beginningcounselor.webs.com) is that I believe we can eventually change this system. Through peer support, accurate, helpful resources, and the power of unity, we can make a difference.

But until the point when the institution of counselor training changes, new counselors are missing out on what they need to SURVIVE and THRIVE in the amazing, challenging and wonderfully unique world of professional counseling.

That's why *The Beginning Counselor's Survival Guide* came into being. What you will find in this book is not more theories. It's not a quick-fix solutions manual, either. It's a practical how-to guide to the day-by-day information you need to grow into the counselor you want to be.

It provides what's been missing from traditional counselor training. The book is divided into three sections, three critical areas that really matter at this stage in your career as a counselor. I call them "core competencies," because it is my belief that these areas must be mastered in order for a new counselor to grow into one who is confident in their vocation.

The first core competency is professionalism. Very, very few graduate programs provide any real help with basic professionalism, as I define it. In my estimation, professionalism is the practice of the laws of one's chosen occupation, as well as the necessary steps that must be taken to master these laws. You know, things like applying for appropriate licensure, setting up an office, working with a supervisor, and more.

The second core area focuses on client relationships. Though most counselors have better-than-average people skills, many begin their careers with no idea how to manage the new challenge of the therapeutic relationship. The counseling relationship has its' own unique rules. These rules aren't terribly hard to master, but new counselors are often not exposed to them early enough in their careers.

The third and most essential core component is counselor self-care. Unfortunately, of all the competencies, it's also the one LEAST likely to be covered in your graduate program. This section focuses on the steps you must take in order to have a long and successful counseling career: developing your own counseling style, planning for your future, and preventing burnout.

I started this book because I was frustrated with the lack of practical education out there. But I kept writing because I got to know many of the new counselors out there and I was inspired by their amazing compassion and hope. I have seen, too many times, new counselors burn out for simple lack of information. When that happens it is not only the new counselors that lose out, but also all the clients that they could have eventually helped.

I was so fortunate in this process. I had a fabulous supervisor, whom you will get to know as the co-author of this book, Dr. Carol Doss. Her insights and witticisms are sprinkled through this book in the form of "Carol's Comments." I've heard a lot of horror stories about bad supervisors, and I always wished I could share my supervisor with the hapless interns in those stories! Through this book, I finally can. I don't think I made it through this process of licensure by accident. I firmly believe that if I hadn't had Carol as my supervisor, I could have <u>easily</u> been one of the disillusioned new counselors left by the wayside.

The Beginning Counselor's Survival Guide was outlined and the majority of it was written while I was still a counselor intern. Through the combination of this perspective (which is also YOUR perspective) and that of a seasoned counselor supervisor with decades of experience, this book will give you everything you need to get licensed and to love your work.

I hope you'll enjoy this book, but most of all that you will benefit from it. I will consider the project a resounding success if "just" one person feels more confident in their abilities after reading it. I want to continue to support you personally, so I invite you to come and join the BeginningCounselor website at www.beginningcounselor.webs.com. It's a free social networking website where you can read helpful articles, connect with other new counselors, and share ideas. I strongly encourage you to subscribe to the BeginningCounselor mailing list as well. Mailing list members get exclusive access to the new counselor chat room, and advance knowledge of freebies and special deals from leading counselor educators, coaches and mentors. Mailing list members will also receive the bi-monthly Question & Answer column chock-full of tips, tricks, and answers to your most pressing concerns.

Also available along with this book is *The Beginning Counselor's Survival Guide Workbook*. Though either can be used independently, the workbook enhances the book's content by providing step-by-step worksheets and tips that correspond with the chapters of the book. You can find out how to order your instant .pdf download by flipping to the last page of this book.

If you absorb only one piece of information from the following material, have it be this: You, beginning counselor, have something special to offer, something that no one else has. I believe in you. Thanks for letting me be a part of your life. I can't wait to see what you do next!

Sincerely,
     Stephanie Ann Adams

TABLE OF CONTENTS

CORE COMPETENCE ONE: PROFESSIONALISM

CHAPTER ONE
SITE SEARCH

This is it! You've finally achieved a level of education that will allow you to put aside some of the classroom work and begin the practice of counseling. Many rewarding things are coming your way, not the least of which is the ability to tell your concerned relatives that their perpetual student is now finally working a "real" job.

A lot of things are running through your head right now. Do I have what it takes to be a successful counselor? Will I pass my NCE? Will I find a job after my internship? These kinds of questions are completely normal. But you need to put all but one of those things aside for the moment. (I promise, we will get back to the rest later.) The one thing that has to be top priority upon starting out is finding a place to host your fledgling counseling skills: a site. A site is fundamental to your new career as a beginning counselor.

WHY DO I NEED A SITE?

To answer that question most simply, counseling students must have an internship or practicum site because it is not legal for them operate independently. Practicum students do not have their degree yet, and clinical interns only have what is called a "temporary" or "provisional" license. There will be more on the difference between the practicum and internship later, but for now it is sufficient to say students need a site because they are in the infancy of their career. A site provides a location for them to begin testing their wings.

Other benefits a site often provides are:

- A physical location to meet clients.
- An office to conduct sessions.
- Clients to work with, or at the very least an established venue to refer them to.
- A site supervisor.

- Administration, such as phone services and filing systems.
- In some cases payment for your time and services.
- Specialized equipment and meeting places such as group therapy rooms, play therapy rooms, and art or music therapy equipment.
- And of course, a real-life model of the counseling profession in action.

The last point encompasses the greatest benefit to be gained from a practicum or internship site. No classroom experience can replicate a day in the counseling field. This will be the first chance to see if you're ready for the life of a professional counselor. It will help you explore your particular calling within the counseling field and decide if that is the right area for you to focus on. It will change your life.

LEARNING THE LINGO: PRACTICUM VS. INTERNSHIP

Practicum. Internship. What's the difference? A lot, as I came to find out the hard way! I had only a vague idea how to describe exactly what I was looking for when I started looking for a site. As a result, many of the counseling organizations I called were very confused about my needs. It ended up delaying my placement and frustrating me to no end! Here's what you need to know in order to not make the same mistake:

> *Carol's Comments*
> Consider sites that will give you a variety of types of clients to see what you like best. You may enjoy working with a different population or age group than you've thought. A variety of client ethnicities or ages can help you realize your strong points.

Your practicum is the course taken usually the last two semesters of your graduate degree. It will be focused more intensely on the actual experience of conducting a counseling session than anything else in the class work prior to it. As part of the requirements for completing this course, you will spend a certain number of hours doing counseling. Usually some of these hours (or all) must be video or audio recorded for classroom and supervisor perusal.

As a practicum student, you have no official title. You are there to learn by doing. You must have an on-site supervisor for your work there, but for some aspects of your learning your professor or the counseling program director at school may also be considered your supervisor. It is more likely than not that you won't be paid for practicum work. Sorry.

When you are on the phone with a potential site or site supervisor, the correct terminology to use when referring to yourself is "practicum student." The people at the sites you will be calling have likely been through counseling training before, and even if you reach someone with a different background, like the receptionist or a child advocate, that is the way they will best understand your status. This label conveys the message that you don't have a degree yet and this will be your first time doing face-to-face counseling. It also tells them you will not require as many hours as a counselor intern and that you need a shorter time commitment than an intern would require.

An intern, on the other hand, has completed a master's or doctoral degree and is temporarily licensed by the state to operate as a counselor under supervision.

There is one big glaring exception I need to note before I proceed: there are some programs in which a student does complete one or more "internships" before graduation in addition to practicum work. This seems to be most common in school counseling and when the student is seeking additional credentials, such as certification as a play therapist. If this is the case for you, please read the rest of this section with the understanding that in my wording a **pre-masters** internship is functionally equivalent to a practicum. If you're seeking pre-masters internship placement over the phone, just make sure you are clear that you're working towards a degree and not (right now) towards licensure.

Both interns and practicum students require liability insurance in order to practice. However, often as a practicum student, your tuition will cover insurance costs. As an intern you're solely responsible for the premium.

As a state-licensed intern you are allowed to use a title to refer to yourself on business cards or in professional correspondence. This title is different from the one you will receive as a fully licensed counselor. For example, in Alabama, the intern is called an "Associate Licensed Counselor."

In my state of Texas, the independent licensure title is Licensed Professional Counselor. For those still under supervision, we tack on the word "Intern" to the title. (LPC-Intern) The reason why it is done this way is so important because it is *unethical to represent yourself as anything more than what you are.* In fact, right before I started my internship, the rules were changed regarding this title. Previously, we were allowed to use "LPCI" as a designation of our status, but it was found that the letter alone at the end wasn't enough. Clients didn't know what that meant. So, as long as I was an intern I was required to always represent myself with a combination of the initials and the last word, like this: LPC-Intern.

> PRACTICUM
> Fewer Hours, Pre-Graduation, No License, No Title, Less Likely To Be Paid
>
> INTERNSHIP
> More Hours, Post-Graduation, Must Have Temporary License, Titled, More Likely To Be Paid

Some other terms you might hear are: Registered Intern, Post-Graduate Intern, Clinical Intern, Counselor Intern or Student Counselor, among others. Other counseling disciplines will use different terms, changing the description to suit the type of study. For example, you might be an MFT-Intern, School

Counseling Intern, or Licensed Chemical Dependency Counselor Intern. Then, of course, if you are training for one specific type of job, you might have a certain kind of title there, such as Advocacy Intern Therapist, or Caseworker. Here's the bottom line: **check your state and know your status.**

Then you can introduce yourself as whatever you are with confidence!

BEFORE YOU LOOK

Some practicum students seem to think that the perfect counseling site is just lying around waiting to be picked up, like a quarter at the beach. Unfortunately, you will need a little bit more than a metal detector to find the right site for you.

I'd firmly recommend before you start calling around looking for sites that you research and compile a "master list" of sites to contact. It's tempting to think, "but what if I do all this work and the first person I call accepts me?" I know. It's fun in the sparkly happy land where everything works out right the first time. But it's just not very likely to happen in real life.

> *Carol's Comments*
> *Think of your site search as practice for when you start looking for a professional job. Remember – whether or not you're accepted at a site probably has more to do with the site's needs than anything about you. Even counselor gender may be considered, depending on the site.*

In finding an internship or practicum site, you are most definitely in a time crunch. Some sites only look for interns at certain times of the year, and practicum students must have a site before too far into their practicum semester or else they'll be forced to drop the class. Don't think this can't happen to you. A student at my school, who started the program the same time I did, ended up being dropped by his site right before we were supposed to start as a group into our practicum class. He had to wait and delay his graduation another semester because he didn't have

5

the practicum site secured before the class started. Graduate schools don't exclude people like my fellow student to be cruel, but they simply cannot work with a student to teach skills as a practicum counselor if the student is not actually seeing clients.

So, with this in mind, it is more advantageous for you to have several interviews and more than one potential offer. Not only that, but it also gives you more opportunities to find the site that's best for you.

Another good reason to make a list is if you're like me and get a little nervous when cold-calling people. After you call two or three people in a row, you will develop a rhythm, and it will get much easier to make those difficult calls. Trust me, for those of us who are more shy with job-seeking, it will make it so much easier to "get it over with" in one sitting than to call at random.

Having a master list allows you to come back to it for reference if you need to make a follow-up call to a particular site and forgot the phone number. As you come across further site possibilities, you can scan through the list to see if you've already called the site while looking somewhere else. The list can also serve as a first-round elimination for unsuitable prospects. For example, if you know you can't work nights, and a particular site requires that, don't even write it down.

The final stop on the train is the telephone call. Unless a particular site stresses that they only accept e-mail communication, DO NOT use it. It is so much easier to get an answer via telephone conversation than email, and it is much more professional. Even though you will still be a student when you start looking for your practicum site, searching for an internship should be treated like a search for a job. Request to speak with the person in charge, and if you are lucky enough to get an interview, show up on time and be professionally dressed. The more seriously you take this process, the more seriously potential sites will consider you.

HOW TO LOOK FOR A SITE

Most schools, thankfully, will have a resource list of potential sites that their students have used before and with which the school has a positive relationship. This is the place to start and will make your site search easy – if you are the first to call!

Here's the thing about school site lists: invariably, some of the information is outdated or incorrect from the previous year. In addition to that, the number of students needing sites is usually larger than the number of sites on the school's resource list. You do the math.

Outside of a school list the easiest way to start a site search is to go on the Internet and search "counseling" and your zip code. It will come up with several sites to start off your list close to your area. You can also add additional elements to your search: "crisis counseling," "play therapy," "animal-assisted therapy," "addiction center" and your zip code. And don't forget to check the phone book for listings of counselors and facilities in your local area.

Internship locator websites might also offer sites that are prepared to take on counseling interns, but when I did some practice searches they didn't have anything in my area and very little to offer for counseling in general. I think the problem is that counseling sites just don't tend to advertise their internships. Counseling facilities don't have the staff and resources to advertise for interns, and let's face it, we need them more than they need us. So try these if you like, but don't expect a whole lot.

A more concentrated form of a search would be to use a therapist finding tool like PsychologyToday.com's Find A Therapist search engine. I might be a little biased about it since I've been listed on it before, but I think the number of therapists and clients that also benefit from it speaks for itself. It's well organized, with all the pertinent information up front – phone numbers, addresses – with room for a personal statement by each therapist. This will help you see what kind of person you might be working under. You can also search different kinds of facilities with different specialties, and search therapists by specialties.

Lastly, don't underestimate the power of networking. If you know someone who recently graduated and is working as a counselor, ask him or her for referrals or tips. If your cousin's friend is a counselor, see if they will call and recommend the counselor accept you as a staff intern. Talk to your church, your high school, and your doctor's office, and try to find someone who can put in a good word for you. Some will say no, but you never know! One of these people might just be the "in" you need to get started.

QUESTIONS TO ASK

You have found a site that wants to meet with you. You are excited and nervous, and not sure what to wear. But remember that even though the site is considering whether or not to accept you, you are doing the same thing with them. There are a lot of options as far as site types, as we will see in the next chapter. Not all of them will be ideally suited to your needs as a practicum student or intern.

In some ways it might seem like you had better accept *any* site that offers you a position. You do have to get those hours in, one way or another. It may come to the point in which you do only have one option. In order to start the semester on time, you may feel you have to take it. But before you take that step, you will need to make sure the proposed site can meet your basic site requirements. If not, it would be a pointless exercise for both you and the site to continue a working relationship. In order to differentiate

> *Carol's Comments*
> You don't have to take whatever site you can find. Make sure it's a good fit for you and does the kind of therapy that interests you.

effectively between the sites that will work and those that won't, I suggest that you start with a rough idea of which are the crucial questions (aka deal breakers) and which are the mere "wants."

One more thing: even though I encourage you to ask as many questions as possible, beware of one thing. Before you ask questions in an interview, make sure you do the research. If you waste time during your interview asking questions that are clearly answered on the counseling site's website or phone book ad, it will look like you don't care. And you *do* care. You care very much!

How many hours can you offer me as a practicum student/intern?

As an intern in Texas I had to accrue 3000 clock hours, 1500 of which had to be face-to-face counseling sessions. As a practicum student, my school required 300 hours total, again half of which had to be face-to-face. Your site must be able to meet your needs in regards to hours or else you will have to add another site to make up the difference. How many hours do you need?

Do you supply clients for your practicum students/interns, or do you require students to find their own?

It never occurred to me that as a complete novice, I might be expected to bring in my own clients to counsel right off the bat. Regardless, several people in my practicum class ended up at sites that expected them to do this. This factor directly impacts your ability to deliver on the hours required for graduation and/or licensure. You must consider carefully whether you will be realistically prepared to take on the challenge. If you do choose to contract with a site that requires you recruit your own clients, read my section on marketing as soon as possible.

Do you have a supervisor on-site, or would I have to find my own?

Seems obvious, but trust me, you'll want to ask.

What are my (prospective) supervisor's credentials?

> *Carol's Comments*
>
> *Trust your gut. Not every supervisor is terrific. If you don't feel comfortable (or sort of comfortable) with this person, keep looking.*

In order that you get credit for your hours, your supervisor must almost always be specially approved as a counselor supervisor. You can look up any counselor or counselor supervisor on your state licensing board to see if they have any violations on record. And you should do that.

How much is the supervision fee?

Check the supervision chapter for details on how supervisor pay structures work. Keep in mind that usually state requirements dictate at least one supervision session per week. That can add up pretty quickly. Still, you have to have supervision, so build it into your budget.

> *Carol's Comments*
>
> *Insurance companies do not reimburse for services performed by unlicensed counselors. The sites themselves can be squeezed in getting no funding (unless by grant or government program), but are expected to train you without billing for your services. This isn't fair for anyone, but it's reality.*

Will I be paid or a volunteer?

It is far easier to find a site that will take you on for free plus a supervision fee, than one that will pay you. I think It's fair to expect that almost no practicum services you provide will be paid. You don't have a degree to offer, and you don't have the flexibility you will have if interning is your full-time job. After you graduate though, it's a different story. I personally don't understand how people expect counselor interns to accrue the kind of hours they need to apply for licensure without being paid, but some sites still are indignant when you ask for compensation for your work. If you are lucky enough to be supported by a spouse or parent during your time of internship, then you have the luxury of accepting an unpaid position. Otherwise, you'll probably have to decline sites that aren't offering payments to their interns. Or take a second job.

Even at the paid sites – I have to be honest here - it's not going to be a good living for a while. The reason it's so hard to earn an adequate amount is that interns usually can't accept insurance, and aren't credentialed to the degree where they can charge a whole lot per session. That doesn't make for a good income. However, after you finish, the situation will get better. No one gets into this job to be wealthy, but after your internship you should be able to take care of your needs and at least help support a family. In my opinion, this career is what you make of it.

> *Carol's Comments*
> Remember this is part of your education, not an actual paying job. The site is helping you even if they're not paying you.

If you are going to be paid, all the usual questions related to money apply. Will I be paid by the hour or by a salary? How often will I be paid? How would I file my taxes? And so on...

What kind of counseling happens here?

Will you be seeing couples, individuals, or adolescents? How long does a typical session last? Will you be expected to do group counseling? Art therapy? Agencies often have specific methods of counseling that they will expect you to comply with. This may be a part of their vision, or simply what they are required to do based on the guidelines of the insurance they accept. Either way, you have to plan on following their rules.

Every site also has some semblance of a theoretical orientation. For example the "Adlerian Center for Family Therapy" will follow Alfred Adler's ideas about emotional wellness and healing. So you will want to ask your site if you will be expected to adhere to a site's main theory (such as Adlerian therapy) strictly, or if there is room for your individual approach.

By the way, when your interviewer asks you, as they will, what your theoretical orientation is, do not say eclectic. While everyone today is eclectic in reality, saying it makes you look wishy-washy. Counselor supervisors tend to hate it. Just say your primary orientation and pull out a few things you like about other theories, if you must.

Who are my clients?

"Which categories of people make up my major demographic?" Is it kids, adolescents, or the elderly? Are the people you will see women, men, or both? What ethnic groups, income brackets, and religious preferences dominate the population? Knowing what kind of person you will be counseling helps you to be sensitive to their particular needs.

How much counseling will I be able to do in proportion to case management or paperwork?

An agency, or any type of practice that takes insurance, will have paperwork. Social work-type sites and domestic violence shelters especially are known for this. However, usually at least half of your total hours for state licensure have to be with clients in counseling, not case management. Consider the amount of paperwork when choosing whether or not to accept them as a site.

How will I be supervised?

In addition to reporting on difficult cases in supervision sessions, your supervisor will most likely wish to have another way of monitoring your progress. There's nothing personal in this. Remember that he or she is liable if you get sued, so they need to be aware of what's going on.

Some of the methods your supervisor may choose to utilize are video and audiotapes, direct observation, observation through a one-way mirror, and counseling together in a group setting. Audiotapes are probably the most common method, and the least intrusive for your client. My school required that videotapes be submitted to view and critique in our practicum class. Sounds daunting, but in the end it was a really effective teaching tool. Remember: *Any video or audiotaping must be done with the full written consent and awareness of the client.* No hidden cameras should ever be used.

When I was in my practicum, my clients were handed an authorization form at intake explaining that I might be using tapes. Even though I had the signatures on file for each of my clients, I reminded clients on the days I would be taping them and reassured them that they had the right to tell me again if they weren't comfortable with it. No grade in class is worth making a client feel threatened in counseling. Despite my worries that they would decline, more often than not it wasn't the issue I thought it would be.

Whether you use video or audio, it is your responsibility, not your site's, to see that all tapes you have made during session are destroyed at the end of the semester. How would you feel if your secrets were on record somewhere and you entrusted them to another person's care? Protect your client and get rid of them properly.

I don't think it is common practice to have your supervisor sit in on sessions with you, simply because he or she is a very busy person already, but it might happen. One of my co-interns at the Family Counseling Center, Brooke, shared a story in a group supervision in which it happened to her. She was working a school counseling job at that time, and was observed directly in play therapy sessions. Her supervisor was also trying to counsel another child in the same room at the time. It was very distracting to the children and to Brooke and ultimately proved to be not a great match for her.

If this is how your site desires to conduct supervision of you, I would carefully consider the possible negative impact this might have on your counseling ability. If a supervisory counselor is in the room with you while you're counseling, you will be more flustered and the client will not know whether they should speak to you or to the counselor supervisor. If this scenario comes up in your interview, you might ask why your potential supervisor feels this is preferable to another method of supervision.

> *Carol's Comments*
> *If a client freaks out and seems really uncomfortable with taping (even after you've explained that it's really for your benefit and you'll be the one being judged) you're better off not taping.*
> *The more matter-of-fact you are in the taped session, the more likely your client is to forget the tape altogether.*

For the same effect but less distraction, another choice might be observation through a one-way mirror. Many sites use this, and it can be useful outside of the supervision process as well. Our play therapy room at the Center has a one-way mirror, and play therapy was something I really wanted to learn about. I was able to observe many sessions of play therapy conducted by experienced interns and LPCs and hone my expertise in that area. Which brings me to the next question I would ask.

How do you feel about my observing you (or another counseling professional employed at this location) in session to learn more about a particular type of therapy?

As I stated previously, one thing I really wanted to become proficient in during my practicum and internship was play therapy. Dr. Roger Doss, the executive director of the center, received his PhD at UNT with Dr. Garry Landreth, a play therapist who is legendary in the field. I was able to observe sessions guided by Roger and other interns already trained in play therapy through our one-way mirror.

> *Carol's Comments*
>
> *Try new things. Isn't that what you're suggesting to your clients?*
>
> *Stretch your comfort zone a little, whether that be in the age range you see or in the counseling techniques you use.*

Is there an opportunity for me to create and lead groups of my own?

This also tests your site's devotion to developing you as a counselor. I do believe that most people who choose to be licensed as a supervisor primarily do so because they enjoy nurturing and training

15

others. But if you are dealing with a site that doesn't have a supervisor on staff, they may be less interested in this process. You just never know. Perhaps they would enjoy someone taking the initiative. Why not ask them and see?

What do you focus on developing in your supervisees as far as therapeutic skills?

I believe this coincides with the previous question in that it is about what you will learn as a result of contracting with this site. You will be able to tell from the interviewer's answer whether their desires correspond with or enhance your own.

What will the hours be?

Can I set my own? Will there be situations in which I need to be "on-call?" Is it nine-to-five? Saturday mornings? Overnight? If you have a family, another job, or like sleeping, you will need to know what your site expects of their interns as far as hours worked. You should expect crisis centers, hospitals, and residential treatment centers to have odd hours and certain times you might need to be on call. Agencies will probably have set office hours with the potential for you to sometimes put in additional hours here and there. In private practice, you might set your own hours completely, or your supervisors might request that you inform them of your available times. In the latter case, they then fill those available times for you in accordance with client availability.

Another question you might add on to that one is: if you are on-call, how much do they expect you to interact with clients over your private phone line? If a potential site demands that you be accessible to clients or staff for an excessive amount of time over the phone, I wouldn't think it would be unreasonable to question if they will provide you some kind of stipend for the additional charges you might incur on your phone bill.

Are you open to a practicum student continuing to work here as an intern after graduation?

For me, this was a pretty important question. It wasn't absolutely necessary, but I like staying put when I find someplace I enjoy. And by the point at which I had my practicum interview, I knew the heartache of scrambling for a site. I was very invested in not having to repeat the process in a year's time. For me, it worked out, and I stayed on after practicum to finish my internship.

Even if you don't know if you will be able to take it now or not, it's good to know if there is a possibility.

Is there a specific length of time you usually take interns for?

The purpose behind this is to discover if you have a chance at coming in right away or if you will have to wait till the next "hiring cycle." Some of the practicum sites I contacted over the latter half of the summer said to "call back in December." It also answers the question of whether or not your period of service ends after a certain amount of time has passed. If it will end before you have accomplished the hours you needed, you're in trouble.

What will be discussed during supervision sessions?

Case studies are to be expected. But there is always more to it than that. Will you be able to volunteer information? Will your supervisor ask you specific questions? Will you have forms to turn in? Are you able to ask questions or expected to mostly listen to a lecture-style delivery?

How many interns do you take on at a time?

This question helps you find out exactly how thinly stretched your potential supervisor might be among needy novices. How long might it take to get an audience should you need one? Or, conversely, if you are the only intern the place supports, how much of a burden will that place on you?

> **Carol's Comments**
> States typically have a number of interns one supervisor can have.

How much group time versus individual counseling time?

Most states will only allow so many group counseling hours to be counted towards your total number of face-to-face counseling hours. You will need to know if your potential site could give you enough individual hours to qualify for graduation or licensure.

> **Carol's Comments**
> Make sure the site can meet your needs as to client hours.

How much group supervision time versus individual supervision time?

It's the same situation here as it is with counseling hours. There is a limit to group supervision hours; a certain number of them must be one-on-one with your supervisor.

How should I stay in contact with my supervisor?

Will you only see your supervisor once a week at supervision? What about questions that come up after that? And of course, what if you need to consult with your supervisor in a truly dire situation? You need to find out what your supervisor would recommend, and who might be a second person to consult if they are not available for a time.

Though Dr. Carol Doss was my clinical director and supervisor, I have discussed some situations with Dr. Roger Doss when I was unable to reach her on a day I had fairly urgent questions. He was just as qualified to answer the question for me as his wife, and he was available at that time.

For emergencies, I have consulted Carol in-office and called her at home. She was understanding and supportive of doing so, as these instances were truly urgent situations. What would your supervisor recommend in cases like these?

> *Carol's Comments*
> Even if you're desperate for a site, make sure you're comfortable with both the supervisor and the clientele served. This is huge. If you're going to take risks in your internship and learn, you need to feel comfortable with where you are.

Final Question to Consider

Will this internship opportunity adequately prepare you for licensure and the plans you have for your career after your internship?

CHAPTER TWO
SITES UNLIMITED

TRADITIONAL

When a person speaks of a "counseling site," probably the typical idea that comes to mind is the stand-alone counseling center model. The site I used for my practicum and internship falls into that category. It's a privately run, not-for-profit group office consisting of two PhD counselors and a rotating number of interns. Outside of the offices of my supervisor, Dr. Carol Doss and her partner and husband, Dr. Roger Doss, there are several offices open for interns, a staff kitchen, a receptionist's desk, a filing office, and a play therapy room. There are two waiting areas and the building has other rooms that can be rented out or used for other purposes. Theirs is probably a pretty typical setup, and it worked great for me. However, as we will soon cover, there are many, many other options available.

> *Carol's Comments*
> *Beginning counselors may not yet know what specialty they prefer, if any. Doing your internship in a larger group that will give you exposure to multiple services might be worthwhile.*

Traditional counseling centers are unlikely to provide crisis services or 24-hour availability. This will be preferable for those of you desiring more "regular" working hours and who are unable to provide "on-call" services.

Solo practice counselors may also at times choose to incorporate interns into their office. Should they agree to take on an intern, that intern would share the office space the counselor rents with them, generally 1-2 session rooms and a seating area. This setup has the benefit of being a more private and intimate setting. The downside is that offices of this size often cannot support staff for answering phones and authorizing payments, so that may be something their intern is required to take charge of for themselves. For the more experienced counselor, I would argue that it is necessary to have a good handle on the administrative side of things, but for beginners it can be overwhelming to take on the whole process at once! Other interns might also prefer to keep the therapeutic experience separate from the administrative one. It's a matter of personal preference.

While these individually practicing counselors may have specific therapeutic tools available for interns to use, this type of site is not likely to have the space for play or group therapy. I have noticed in my research that many counselors who work individually tend to emphasize one particular service within or in addition to general counseling services: hypnosis, weight control behavior modification, and the like. It makes sense, as each counselor should find a way to make the treatment they offer distinctive from their competitors. But that may require that an intern focus exclusively or primarily on that service as well, which may be too narrow for their interests at this point in their career.

While every situation is different, most of the single-office counselors I spoke to when looking for my internship site were not prepared to take on the responsibility of an intern. Some even seemed surprised I was asking! One reason for this may be lack of space, but another might be that the law requires interns to be supervised by a licensed or otherwise state-endorsed counselor supervisor. This is a special designation outside of the qualifications required of a licensed professional counselor. For smaller places, pursuing supervisor status often isn't really in the scope for the vision that counselor has for their business.

In cases like these you may still be allowed to work at one place and have a supervisor that works elsewhere, as long as that supervisor agrees in writing to take on the responsibility for you working at that site. (Check with your state counseling board!) I'll tell you more about supervisor's responsibilities later.

MEDICAL

Another place that can work as an internship site but may not provide a counselor supervisor on-staff is a hospital or medical facility. Medical sites occasionally use counselors for bereavement and pain management counseling and it is possible to count those hours towards your licensure goals. Of course, the situations you would end up dealing with would be rather limited, but at the same time you would be developing a specialty that could be used later on to market yourself. At hospitals, bilingualism is a plus and the hours may be more irregular.

A private mental hospital or the mental health ward of a general hospital may also be a potentially fruitful site to work from. Financial compensation for hours spent as an intern counselor is often difficult to find. However, employment as a psychiatric aide, or "psych tech," *is* paid and does allow accumulation of counseling hours. These types of places are likely to offer group counseling to their patients, and possibly individual counseling as well. An intern in a mental hospital will have to be more vigilant in making sure they have opportunity for hours since no college degree is required for the job, making the psychiatric aide who is looking to become a counselor an anomaly rather than a common occurrence.

Most of the work as a psych tech is taking care of suicidal or seriously mentally ill patients' physical needs, such as bathing, helping them eat or put on clothes. If you have physical difficulties yourself, this is probably not the job for you because you must be able to restrain patients who are dangerous to themselves or others, as well as support a patient's weight when taking care of them. There is much opportunity for interaction with the patient, but the nature of the interaction may quite different from that with outpatient clients. However, psych techs are the ones who get the most time and experience with a particular patient. It might be a great opportunity to hone your observation and diagnostic skills by recording and reporting on patient behaviors to treatment staff.

Whether drug and alcohol addiction is your specialty or you are simply looking for options, addiction centers also make reliable and interesting work sites. In addition to group counseling, many recovering addicts are required to attend individual counseling sessions on-site – with counselors like you! Addiction work is more specialized, but at the same time, everyone there has a history that led up to this point. You won't be "just trying to help them stop using", as some might fear, you will be plumbing their past for factors leading to their drug use and helping them set up methods to keep themselves clean. Additional or alternate licensure/certification in substance abuse counseling is available if you find you like this line of work.

CRISIS CARE

Domestic violence shelters and help centers are a major employer of counseling students and interns, most likely because the need is so great and fresh counselors have such a yearning to help others. This is also usually in an office setting, although sometimes you might be asked to go to the shelter itself to visit a woman who has just come in. I have heard from my friends in the business that space can be rather crowded in a domestic violence help center, and they may find themselves squeezed in an office the size of a broom closet and negotiating time there with a dozen other interns! But despite that, they feel very useful to be dealing with such an immediate problem. Domestic violence centers tend to emphasize intake forms and be particular with paperwork, and in many cases each client is limited to a certain number of sessions with any counselor, whether student or licensed. While the main population served will be women, sometimes the children and teenagers exposed to violence will need help as well.

Speaking of children, I had a chance in my own site search to look closely at a children's advocacy center. This particular center offered group therapy, counseling individually for parents, and in many cases forensic interviews on-site. (I should note that any intern counselor is not likely to be allowed to conduct these interviews, used for court cases, but it is a priceless opportunity for observation.)

The purpose of advocacy centers is to pinpoint cases of child abuse and protect the child or children involved to the best of their ability. They work closely with the legal system, which can sometimes be frustrating to a counselor's purposes, as the law seeks justice, and counselors seek healing. They are not always the same thing. But working alongside legal processes can also feel very rewarding if and when "right is done." There will be a high volume of children you will be able to help, but along with that a great deal of sad stories and shattered families. It is never easy to see people suffering, but seeing a child suffer is different than seeing an adult suffer because adults have choices that help them get out of their situations. Children often don't. Be aware of the emotional challenges when seeking an internship in this type of site.

Reproductive health centers, such as Planned Parenthood and crisis pregnancy services, employ counselors to help the women and their partners or families deal with reproductive challenges. This can be a sensitive issue, and you will want to consider your personal stance on the options you'll be asked to provide at each place. There is nothing wrong with saying you can't be objective on this issue, but not if you're going into a position that requires objectivity! I have a hunch that it will probably be easier for female counselors than for male counselors to get positions in these organizations, but you never know. Your time there is likely to be short except in rare occasions. If the client is working through issues outside reproductive choices and challenges, you will probably be asked to refer them out.

If you're a type that thrives under pressure, a crisis call line or rape crisis center may be the place for you. This kind of job usually requires specialized training in interventions outside of "regular" counseling techniques, which may feel constricting to those who have been enjoying working with a certain theoretical orientation in school. The hours are more unpredictable in this type of work, and it is much easier to get involved with crisis counseling as a volunteer than a paid employee.

As you can imagine, the potential for burnout is high. You will at times come to work in the middle of the night, and routinely see people immediately post-trauma. It can take a toll on your personal life, as you might have to be "on call" at late or odd hours. There might be some issues as well with qualifying the hours spent on the phone at a hotline as "counseling hours." Most states stipulate that at least a third of the hours required for licensure be face-to-face, and phone counseling might not suffice. Be aware of the challenges before you agree to take on the job.

> **Carol's Comments**
> One aspect of effective supervision is that the supervisor needs to help you be aware of your own reactions. Self-care should be addressed.

One of the more out-of-the-ordinary settings among the very diverse group of potential counseling sites is that of the residential treatment facility. As issues like eating disorders, cutting, and adolescent chemical dependency have risen, so have locations geared to meet the needs of those in this type of crisis. These will not be located in every U.S. town and often require live-in staff, as their goal is to provide structure and consistency for troubled youth. Obviously, this can be ideal for the single person, but cause difficulties for those with families. It can be intense and high-stress, and most of the people there will probably not want to be in anyone's care. Regardless, like crisis work, it provides an immediacy of relationship. This might be ideal for those who despise routine and stagnation. However, if you like waking up knowing what's going to happen in your life each day, try something else.

There's a lot to consider with this kind of site. But the fact remains: crisis work is very exciting. It can also be intensely rewarding when you are someone's lifeline at a time when everything is at stake. It can remind you that you're alive, and create a feeling of purpose that's hard to duplicate in "regular" work. An option to manage the potential for high stress might be to make this a part-time pursuit, dedicating only certain days, and not the majority of your week or month, to crisis work.

SPIRITUAL

Churches, synagogues, and other religious facilities can sometimes support counselor interns as well. This is where it is important to be careful that you have the proper supervision, as pastoral counselors and Biblical counselors will not be considered sufficiently credentialed to provide intern supervision. You can resolve that by talking to your supervisor. Simply ask your supervisor if he or she would agree to provide supervision and be responsible for your actions on this additional site. If they agree to support you, get the agreement *in writing* and then submit it to your state licensing board for approval.

Churches are a great place to get started and can be easy to get into if you have a relationship with the staff or are a member of the congregation. The challenge with church counseling consists primarily of the century-long disagreement between psychology and organized religion. Some Christians believe it is not trusting God to go to a counselor for help with their problems, and if you are going into this setting you must be prepared to defend yourself (kindly, of course) against this type of objection. Another issue of concern would be the ethical issue of dual relationship, meaning outside of just being the person's counselor, it is likely you will also be their fellow church member or work in the nursery together! You must consider for yourself how you will keep the professional relationship separate from any personal relationship.

Others in the church may also feel entitled to question you about what your client talks about in session. They might feel that the camaraderie of shared faith and friendship gives them the right to know, but the rule of confidentiality still applies. Unless the person you are counseling chooses to share or releases you in writing to disclose information, you cannot break their confidentiality.

Sometimes, if you spend your internship or otherwise advertise yourself as a "Christian counselor," people not of your faith may find it uncomfortable to go to you. If it is your plan anyway to be known as a Christian counselor, this will not be an issue, but if you want a wider range of clients, you might consider another path.

Lastly, there will be some clients who feel it is "un-Christian" for you to accept payment for providing them support. You must make the distinction with them that you are asking for compensation for the benefit of your training, not just your support, and that this is how you make a living. In my experience, if boundaries are clearly stated in any counseling setting, everyone is usually fairly agreeable.

Jewish synagogues are somewhat more difficult places to find intern work when compared to Christian churches. Many Jewish synagogues offer counseling services by the rabbi alone. Counseling students of the Jewish faith *may* be able to find work at a Jewish community services center instead. Some examples of Jewish community services would be Jewish Family Services, Jewish Hospice Care, and Jewish Chaplaincy Services.

Opportunities are beginning to spring up for counselors who wish to work within a Muslim community as well. Private counseling centers and Islamic family services organizations are probably the best place to start if you are looking to practice counseling from an Islamic perspective.

COMMUNITY

Each state should have an organization that serves the community relative to those suffering from developmental disabilities and other challenges with mental health. My local community mental health organization provides care for developmental issues, addiction services, early childhood development intervention and some crisis support. The best part for counseling students is that they often do offer limited paid internships, a godsend for those of us who want to do our internship as our main job. To find a similar organization in your area, search online for "mental retardation services" or "mental health services" along with the name of your state. Counseling individuals with developmental delays requires a different skill set than counseling adults or even children, so be open to adapting your style if you choose this type of internship.

Counseling services for the physically handicapped are an often-overlooked opportunity for student internship. Before embarking on this process it's important to consider reviewing the recent research about counseling those with the disability you would be working with. Lately this area has deservedly been getting more attention and there's an abundance of material out there to work with. Specialized research is essential, because issues with disability are not easily generalized among all disabled persons. An important thing to remember is that even though these individuals are dealing with disabilities, they also have many of the same problems everybody else does: relationship issues, communication problems, the quest for self-actualization, and the like. Let the client define their own goals, and you will be fine.

To find appropriate sites that serve disabled populations, you could start with finding local and state government programs for the disabled. If they don't have a link to counseling services on their website, they can likely tell you over the phone to whom they refer those who need counseling services.

Vocational rehabilitation also serves the handicapped. VR, as it is known, helps veterans with injuries related to military service and those with physical or mental handicaps evaluate their skills, find practical job training or enroll in further schooling. The VR counselors may also oversee specific problems unique to the client's case. These case-specific issues might include things like providing benefits to a company hiring a war vet, or finding medical services to treat an individual's problems. You may need special training or licensure to be a vocational rehab counselor intern, depending on where you intend to practice. This job will require making a good deal of phone calls, working with different agencies and businesses, and administering evaluative tests.

Another source of hours can be with the state prison system. Like the job of a psych tech at a psych hospital, a prison psychology associate is a hybrid job combining order and discipline and therapeutic skills. As the name suggests, this is a job slightly more psychology-based than counseling-based, in that the focus is on creating programs and performing assessments. Sometimes candidates might be limited to solely doctoral psychology students, which would be an issue if that were not your career path.

A liaison therapist, in addition to providing counseling services, organizes early intervention programs, educates on pertinent topics, and develops positive and beneficial relationships with community organizations, such as hospitals, schools and government programs. They are likely to be found working at a government-funded organization or a residential treatment facility on a large scale, but do not seem to be available in high numbers. Unless you have an "in" with a potential liaison therapy job, I would not expect to easily come across one.

Career counselors are found in much greater numbers. A career counseling intern would likely have the opportunity to specialize within a subdivision of vocational therapy, should they so choose. A career counselor's role is to take a client's job history and elicit from them their goals for their career. Your graduate degree course in career counseling probably involved taking standardized tests that match career with aptitude or personality. These are exactly the kinds of tests you will now be administering to your career clients. As a career counseling intern, you would need to utilize a variety of methods of helping your client research new and creative career opportunities. Some career counselors choose to focus on one broad career category, others might choose to open their field up to any and all positions available.

The final incarnation of an internship site I am going to explore might seem a little obvious, but it is worth looking over. If you want understanding from your site, support for your school hours, and immediacy of training, look no further than your own school. That's right. Nearly all (if not all) schools provide counseling services *gratis* to their students. They need individuals to staff these positions, and who better to pull from than their own counseling department?

The advantages can be huge. Your bosses will not want to schedule you during class hours; you will have easy access to your professors, and not have to travel far from your "home away from home" to do your work.

The challenge is that everyone else in your program will likely have the same designs as you do on this precious position! At my school, I think there were two intern positions open for over 100 practicum students, so you can guess that more than a few people were disappointed.

For some, it may be uncomfortable to provide counseling services to your fellow students who will also see you joking around in the hallway or maybe even nodding off in class. Hours are primarily in the evening, as most of your clients will have classes during the day. After all, they are students.

The list of options for counseling sites we've just reviewed may seem daunting, but it should be energizing as well. Whatever your interest, time availability, and background, there is a counseling intern job that will fit you.

CHAPTER THREE
SUPERVISOR SAVVY

WHAT IS SUPERVISION?

Supervision in counseling has a meaning unique among any other uses of the word. A supervisor in the workplace is a dominating force, curtailing your creativity and enforcing the rules. (Or at least that's what many of them *tend* to do.) But a counselor supervisor maintains a balance between leading as a governing force and encouraging as a mentor. Their role is that of both teacher and guardian. They must simultaneously encourage your growth and development *and* protect clients from your mistakes.

Every counseling theory has its own idea of how supervision should be done, and most of these ideas are pretty self-explanatory. For example, Rogerian supervision purports that the most important aspect of supervision is modeling the unconditional positive regard expected of a Rogerian counselor. There are also supervision models that are more eclectic, and those that focus on supervisee development. There is not one preferred model universal to the counseling field, and some supervisors don't really claim any theory of supervision as their own. Familiarize yourself with the options, but unless you want to, you shouldn't have to get bogged down in it.

WHAT TO LOOK FOR IN A SUPERVISOR

This is such a highly subjective category that many of you are probably wondering why I even put it in here. The thing is, no matter what your needs or preferences, there are some things that are absolutely imperative to have in a supervisor.

- Someone in your area of interest. Obvious, right? But it is *so easy* to get desperate in the search to find yourself a supervisor, ANY supervisor, that this little aspect can be overlooked. And this little aspect becomes a big deal when you apply for your independent license, all ready to work with, say, troubled children, but only having had experience with drug and alcohol counseling.

- Someone who you feel comfortable with. During your initial meeting, do they blast questions at you? Do you feel like you're on trial? My supervisor holds all of her interns to high standards, but she never condemns in tone. I respond much better to "that's probably not a good idea" than I do to someone barking condemnation at me. Consider what you can and can't work with. What if a supervisor was rude, sexist or extremely negative? Do you really want to study under that kind of personality for two or more years?

- Someone you respect. You cannot learn from someone you don't respect. I don't care how many degrees they have. You will write off everything they have to say if you don't respect them.

- Someone who encourages you to try new things. Hey, this is it! We've been released onto the playground after years in class without recess! Of course we want to test our wings. A good supervisor encourages you to try the things you're interested in, while overseeing that you are doing it ethically and to the best of your ability.

- Someone who models good boundaries. As we will see in later chapters, boundaries are HUGE when it comes to healthy client-counselor relationships. How can you learn that if your supervisor isn't demonstrating it for you?

- Someone who returns calls and emails. You have to have someone you can count on to be there for you within a reasonable amount of time. You don't know what you're doing on your own – this is why you need a supervisor!

- Someone who leads but doesn't hover. You cannot learn if you're not allowed to try things for yourself. A supervisor should monitor a supervisee's progress and gradually give them more and bigger challenges as their skill set grows.

SUPERVISOR'S RESPONSIBILITIES

The ACA Code of Ethics supplies the best job description I have found for a clinical counseling supervisor. It tells us that a supervisor should teach their supervisee further counseling skills and educate them about what it means to be a counselor. They should do so with an awareness of cultural differences, either between themselves and the supervisee, or between the supervisee and their clients. They inform and encourage ethical counseling practice. To put it very simply, they are your Yoda.

> *Carol's Comments*
> *The best supervisors are those who actually enjoy passing on knowledge. Some people are annoyed by this and may be doing it for reasons other than personal gratification. You're going to benefit most from a learning relationship with someone who enjoys helping train others.*

But for everything a supervisor should do, there are some things that they should absolutely not do. For one, your supervisor should not have dual relationships with you and should keep the boundaries clear. Except for special occasions like weddings or holiday parties, they should not socialize with you outside of the office. This can feel very odd at times because often people that work in the same place will get together afterwards and hang out. That wouldn't be acceptable for a supervisor and supervisee, however. The reason this is a rule is not because your supervisor doesn't like you. It's simply that there's an unfair power differential in your relationship. She (or he) cannot be the equivalent of your "boss" half the time and your BFF the other half. In a way, it can be frustrating, because I had a little hero worship thing going for my supervisor and would have totally loved to be her BFF. But this rule is to protect and preserve your relationship during your practicum and internship. You can still be friendly in the office, and it's okay to talk about what's going on in your lives to some degree. But remember the primary purpose of this relationship is to *mold you into a professional counselor*, and that goal has to be protected.

Along those lines, you cannot have a supervisor you are related to. It's just not objective! It's a firm ethical standard that the person judging you competent for licensure not be the one that, you know, gave birth to you or something.

Continuing the list of unacceptable behavior by a supervisor, your supervisor should not subject you to sexual harassment or have a sexual relationship with you. It's ethically inappropriate.

> **Carol's Comments**
> Supervisors have power over your learning process, but don't give them too much power. They're people and they have challenges and issues, too. The really good supervisors will readily acknowledge this.

Another thing a supervisor is not allowed to do is to provide you with counseling. They help you with so much already, it can be a temptation to take things further and ask for their help with more personal problems as well. The reason why this can't work is, again, the issue of dual relationship. One person can't oversee you as a counselor and be your counselor as well. It causes major problems. The only issues your supervisor can help you with are problems that get in the way of your counseling: countertransference, for example. Everything else needs to remain at the conversational level only.

In the first chapter, I suggested you ask your potential supervisor about ways you can contact them in case of counseling emergency. This is the reason why: because it is only ethical that they do so. They are overseeing you, and you need to be able to find them when you need help. Of course, no one can be available 24-7, but what do you do if you need an answer immediately? I would also expect that they give you a few different ways to reach them with non-emergency information in between supervision sessions. I worked in a relatively small office building, so I had the potential of running into my supervisor almost anytime. But some people may work in different buildings than their supervisor, or even different facilities. It is your supervisor's job to make it clear how you will connect.

Your supervisor should be taking on the responsibility of regularly giving you feedback on your counseling practices as soon as you begin a relationship, along with providing suggestions for how to improve any weaknesses you may have. The best way to make sure this happens is to see your supervisor at your weekly appointments. Don't feel intimidated if there's something specific you want evaluation in. Feel free to ask. This is your one opportunity to have the complete attention of an experienced, trained counselor and you should take advantage of it.

> *Carol's Comments*
> *Resist the tendency to think you should know stuff. After all, your supervisor has much more experience. Be okay with not knowing until you ask.*

The ultimate responsibility of a supervisor is to back up the new counselor with their name and reputation. By taking you under supervision, they are saying: I believe in this counselor's skills and I stand behind their ability. This takes the form of endorsement for licensure, and having their name associated with you in some of the marketing materials you might be putting out. It also involves signing off on judgments you have made about clients the supervisor may not have ever seen. It's kind of a big deal! So make sure you are checking in with your supervisor on a regular basis and asking how you are progressing, because you don't want to be blindsided with a rejection later. If there is something they feel is underdeveloped about your counseling ability, better to know sooner so that you can do something about it.

The final responsibility of a supervisor is to initiate, or allow termination of, a supervisory relationship under certain circumstances. If there is a conflict, they should lead the way in making certain this conflict is given an opportunity to resolve itself. More on that later. There may be more simple reasons the relationship has to end, such as someone moving, having a baby, or maybe retiring. Either way, your supervisor should refer you to another who can provide you with the services you need.

To keep supervisors accountable to these standards, the ACA code states that supervisors should make supervisees aware of where they might lodge a complaint if there is a problem with the supervisor's behavior. You may already know that we are required to inform our clients of this type of information when we begin a counseling relationship with them. Our supervisors are no different in this respect.

FEES AND MEETINGS

Fun fact: Alaskan counseling students are allowed much more leeway in supervision by phone than are other states, for the obvious reason that their population is very spread out. The nearest supervisor might be hundreds of miles away! In most other states, however, the authorities will be much more strict about requiring face-to-face, one-on-one meetings.

In general, you should expect to participate in sessions lasting 50-60 minutes at least once a week, with more time spent one-on-one than time spent in group supervision. It is most common for you to discuss particular cases that are troubling you, although there are usually no restrictions on what counseling-related topics you may discuss. For example, you might talk about changes in counseling regulations that affect interns, general philosophies about a disorder or dysfunction, or agency-wide concerns.

While there is no way to predict exactly the fees you could expect to be charged for a supervisor's services, I have compiled a general overview of fee structures and charges I have personally encountered.

Per-Session: A flat rate per 50-60 minute session. This is comparative to a fee for a licensed counselor's services, most often somewhere between $50 and $150. A supervisor usually provides a per-session fee at a lower price for group supervision, perhaps $50-60, although I have seen as low as $20.

Per-Month: Supervisees can contract with a supervisor for a package per month, which I've seen range from $500-$1500. Usually the pricier ones include something else to set them apart, such as 24-hour-availability for emergencies.

Discounted Bulk: A special rate per chunk of supervisory sessions ordered. This is hard to generalize as far as prices go, but it should end up being less *per* session than if you bought each session individually. For example, if the fee for supervision is usually $60/hour, the bulk rate for 10 sessions might be $500.

Sliding Scale: These supervisors base your fee on your income according to a set formula they have developed. When they work separately from you, they may ask to see proof of income. If you work for them, they may take a fee based on the income you earn at that location.

SURVIVING BAD SUPERVISORS

My supervision experience has been profitable both personally and professionally, and I hope many others can say the same. But I do know that the ideal supervisory relationship is not always the reality that occurs. From my conversations with other interns, I have heard of some unfortunate circumstances. Here are just some of them.

- Lisa accepted a job with the promise of having an on-site supervisor and then later discovered there was no one on-staff qualified to do the job. She wasted a lot of time working for people under false pretenses, and it took her that much longer to accomplish her required internship hours.

- Julie was condemned in a performance review for feeling sad at the separation from her clients after counseling termination. Her school status was jeopardized, over what is ultimately a very normal reaction.

- A domineering supervisor prevented Jeremy from actually having the opportunity to do counseling, instead overloading him with case management or "grunt work." Jeremy paid her for over six months of supervision before he finally gave up on her continued promises to give him the counseling hours he needed after he had a "little more experience."

- Miranda was chastised for working with an agency client on a goal that was not in the treatment plan, despite the fact that it was well within the range of the her capabilities and it was a goal the client desired to accomplish.

- Anthony's supervisor didn't show up for their supervision meetings, and then asked Anthony to lie on his school forms and say that the supervisor was performing his duties as he was supposed to.

While I have tried to keep everyone's privacy by disguising some revealing details, each one of these stories actually happened.

So what do you do when bad supervisors happen to good supervisees? The first thing to do is talk to them. It can be really intimidating to address a problem with somebody in a position of authority over you, but it is only fair to try to talk to him or her about the problem first. They may not even realize what they're doing – shocking as that is. Use "I-statements" to avoid sparking defensive reactions, and when all else fails, play dumb. For example, you might say, "I know you have been busy the past few weeks, but I thought that the rules were we had to have supervision sessions every week." You know what you're saying, and the supervisor knows what you're saying, but you've avoided shaming him or her by calling them out. Though sometimes that might seem like the most desirable choice, you may have no option but to preserve the relationship, and this gives you a way to do it.

This is a very, very delicate situation. You are paying for their services, and they have an ethical obligation to fulfill them as stipulated by the governing authorities. But there is a reason why so many supervisors get away with problem behavior – their supervisees are afraid to say anything because they need those hours so much. Many of them may feel trapped, and decide to grin and bear it, rather than risk losing their site. As we discussed earlier, they're not that easy to obtain! And many students may feel that the stigma of having left another supervisory relationship may haunt them in a future partnership.

I can't make that decision for you. But I want to assure you that you are not without options in this situation. If talking to the supervisor directly fails, try consulting with a professor at school about the problem. They may be able to give you appropriate advice under the circumstances, and if you are still in your degree program, it is possible they may choose to talk to your supervisor on your behalf. If there are other interns under your supervisor's guidance, speak with them about your problems and see if you might be able to unite under a common goal.

If you have to leave the supervisory relationship due to a conflict, your supervisor should, under ethical guidelines, refer you to another supervisor with whom you might be more successful. If they do not do this, or you feel that your conflict has crossed the line from personality difference to ethical violation, contact your state board for an investigation. This is a drastic step and may not always be advisable. Again, this is a decision only you can make.

Carol's Comments:
Think carefully before just taking a recommendation they have offered. If you've had personal or professional conflicts with a supervisor, you might not have a better experience with his friend.

In this situation, I encourage you to be aware of your own power. You do not have to be a victim of bad circumstances. Be proactive in pursuing what you need, bringing client problems to your supervisor's attention, requesting meetings, and pursuing answers until you get them. If you are laboring under unfair expectations, or if you feel you have been sold short in your capabilities, put your case together and discuss it. Consult with others for their emotional support and advice. Document all conflicts and/or violations, and get corroboration where you can. If you make the decision to apply for other jobs, explain the problems you have had previously in matter-of-fact terms. If you avoid vitriol, your prospective new employers will respect your perspective.

Problems such as these are part of the practice of being a professional counselor. In this world, you have to have firm boundaries and respect for your own ability. If you are faced with this situation, it isn't ideal, but it gives you an opportunity to develop character qualities that will benefit you in your future career.

CHAPTER FOUR
APPLYING FOR LICENSURE

GRADUATION! NOW WHAT?

It was May 15, 2009. Graduation day. Everyone kept asking me the same question. "Are you excited? Are you relieved that you're *done*?"

In a word: no.

It was a really invigorating experience, realizing I had earned a master's degree and was probably done with school for a long time, if not forever. But my Counseling MA (like my BA in Family Psychology before it) was functionally useless unless I took the next step.

The academic education, as far as working as a practicing counselor goes, is only Part I. Part II is still ahead: proving your competency to the state. It's just the way things work. You have your degree, but until you have your license, you cannot call yourself a counselor. To help you understand the process a little better, I've provided a typical outline of the journey below.

TIMELINE

Practicum ➔ Graduation ➔ Testing ➔ Application for Temporary License ➔ Approval for Temporary License ➔Internship ➔ Turning in Hours ➔ Full Licensure Granted

This is going to be fairly similar whether you are seeking a professional counselor license, a marriage and family therapist license, or any of the other possible licensures. Do you see why I was a little stymied? Graduation is only the second in a list of nine stages until one can authentically call themselves a Licensed Professional Counselor. So while graduation is awesome, and you should be proud of what you've accomplished, you're not there *quite* yet.

NCE, NCMHCE AND MORE...

The National Counseling Exam is arguably the most commonly used method of verifying counselor proficiency in the United States. Though not yet the gold standard for everyone, it does seem to dominate!

I had all the paperwork ready to go for the NCE the second I got the last thing I needed for my application: a transcript of my degree from my *alma mater*. I have heard of situations where students have been allowed to apply to take the NCE before graduation, but as far as I can tell that is not always possible. Ask your professors and check with the NBCC (National Board for Certified Counselors) to see what's true for your situation. In my case, I called my school and requested the transcript two weeks before my graduation, because I knew my school would be bombarded with such requests immediately after graduation. It made the most sense to get it in early. I mailed off my temporary licensure application with the check as soon as I received the transcript in the mail, which was about 3-4 days after graduation.

The testing board about two weeks later sent me an email with the choices for test dates and locations. I booked a time slot from Florida on the tail end of my honeymoon. Did I mention I was also getting married during the time I was applying to be a counselor intern? I know what you're thinking – that I have the most understanding husband ever. (I do.) But I also really, really wanted to get this thing started. If you're not in as much of a hurry as I was, then don't worry about rushing like I did. The point I want you to take from this story is not to do things my way, but that this isn't a process that goes by quickly. If you want to get this done, you will have to be on top of it.

Graduation was May 15, my wedding was May 30, and I received the email from the testing board the first week of June. The earliest test date I could get from that point was July 7, which I was actually really happy about. (In my state at that time, they *only* gave the NCE during the first week of the month. There was no way I could take it the first week of June, as I was in Florida. So July 7 was actually a good date, even though it was a month away.) I say all this to give everyone an idea of the time it takes to process all these steps. I'll ask you to remember these dates later on in this chapter.

Any kind of standardized test can be really scary. One that decides if you will be allowed to use this degree you just spent thousands of dollars earning is quite *significantly* more intimidating. You will need to take this test seriously. It's a big one (200 questions) and it will take several hours to complete. *But it is doable.* I'm going to tell you how.

Though there are 200 questions, only 160 of them are actually used to determine your score. The rest are used to test for future questions for other hapless intern-wannabes. Though each state determines a different passing score, they are for the most part pretty reasonable numbers, equivalent to around 70-80%. There's no "curve", so you don't have to worry about anyone else taking your spot. It's just about your score, and your score alone.

You have four hours to take the test, and you must go to a pre-approved testing center to take it. They will send you this information when you are approved for the NCE and can register to sit for the exam. You may test along with other candidates taking other exams at the same time, or you may be alone. Though a lot of information online refers to the paper test, it is more likely from what I've been hearing that you will be taking a CBT. (Computer-Based Test) CBTs come with a tutorial on how to use the computer and a function that allows you to mark questions you're unsure about for later review. Best of all, you can learn *that day* whether you passed or failed! Just a few minutes after you notify the monitors that you have finished your test, they should be able to receive your results. Hopefully, they will hand them straight to you with no funny business. The monitor running my testing group thought it was hysterically funny to hold onto the computer printout and pretend he wasn't going to give it to me. At that point, I seriously considered the possibility of committing homicide. But comparatively, I had it easy! If you are taking the paper-based test rather than a CBT, you will have to wait several <u>weeks</u> for the results, which will be mailed to you.

The questions on the test are based on the classes you should have had to take in order to qualify for state licensure: group counseling, helping relationships, research methods, ethics, development, career counseling, social/cultural foundations and testing. The questions also focus on professional practice issues.

There are a lot of different ways to study for a test like this, but here's a few pointers I've picked up that I believe will improve your chances of success.

TESTING TIPS

- Take a bunch of practice tests through an online/computer-based test prep service. They're harder than the real test, and so if you do well on those you're very likely to do well on the real one.
- Get Howard Rosenthal's book *Encyclopedia of Counseling*, 3rd Ed. Funny, educational, and not boring. It's also available on tape. One caveat: those who are not good with multiple-choice questions have reported that they felt this book made the test more difficult. This was not my experience, but just so you are aware.
- Using the online practice tests you've already taken, pinpoint and focus on your two worst areas. Near the end, study the heck out of those, instead of focusing on the content at large. If you're decent

at everything else, it will help the most to study what you don't know well.

If worst comes to worst, you still have options. According to the Texas State Board of Examiners for Professional Counselors, students are allowed to retake the NCE after 3 months has elapsed if they have previously failed it. If the NCE is failed twice, however, the student is required to retake nine hours of graduate work or wait two years before testing again. No, that isn't a pleasant prospect, but at least it is a viable option. It means the door isn't closed.

According to the *Statues and Regulations for Professional Counselors,* Alaska also allows a second retake with 90 days notice and another examination fee. They don't say anything about a third retake. Check your state's policies before you start studying, so you know your fail-safe options.

The other big test that is often used for licensing standards is the NCMHCE, one that I can barely type out without mixing up the acronym. It stands for the National Clinical Mental Health Counselor Examination. (Really? We need *all* of those adjectives?) This is another expression of the effort to nationalize standards for counseling practice, although now it can only prove competency in the states that accept it as a licensing standard.

Though I hate the name, I have to admit I really like the style of the test, which focuses on clinical competency rather than academic ability.

> *Carol's Comments:*
> *Everyone has a unique testing style. Know what works for you and make this your method. Others will tell you how the test is to be taken, but you're hopefully the best judge of your own strengths. Use them.*

> THE TEST CAN BE CONCEPTUALIZED LIKE THIS:
> 10 CASE STUDIES
> ↓
> 5-8 QUESTIONS PER CASE
> EACH QUESTION EITHER
> ↙ ↘
> INFORMATION GATHERING   DECISION MAKING

Information gathering (IG) simply focuses on how well you can assess the facts relevant to the case. Here's an example: if you're examining a diagnosis for a mood disorder, which ones of these items is not relevant? A) Depressed mood most of the day. B) Insomnia. C) Diminished interest or pleasure in all, or almost all activities. D) Client's bank account balance.

I hope you answered D, or else you're in bigger trouble than I know what to do with! You will need to be comfortable with each diagnostic axis of the DSM-IV; however, you shouldn't need to memorize the numbers that go with the diagnosis.

Axis I covers the diagnoses you will probably be most interested in, disorders and conditions like Major Depressive Disorder and Dissociative Identity Disorder. Axis II focuses solely on personality disorders and mental retardation. It might help to think of this axis as the place to classify more permanent disorders, as personality disorders are considered pervasive and lifelong and mental retardation is non-reversible. The third axis is for medical conditions. These are, of

Carol's Comments:
DSM diagnoses are vital to a variety of aspects of therapy. Insurance companies rely on them. Know this manual well. It can get you paid.

course, not our area of expertise, but thankfully the DSM devotes a large portion of the text to listing these disorders with their ICD-9-CM codes. All we have to do is simply record what information a medical doctor has already provided. The fourth axis is labeled "Psychosocial and Environmental Problems." Here is where you note anything else of relevance to the diagnostic decision or understanding of the person's situation that is not placed elsewhere on the axis. For example, an ugly divorce and custody battle would be relevant in the diagnosis of a child with Oppositional Defiant Disorder. Job stress or job loss can be relevant for a person with an anxiety disorder. Finally, Axis V asks you to rate your client on the Global Assessment of Functioning (GAF). Check the DSM for specific definitions, but as a general rule if a person scores lower than 50 they're not functional, as most people would define it. (American Psychiatric Association, 1994)

Decision-Making (DM) is based on using this information to make clinically sound judgments about interventions you might use on this client. It might sound intimidating, but I actually think it might be rather fun. I didn't take the NCMHCE, but some of the practice tests I took online in my research were enjoyable! These are very useful skills to have, and so studying for this kind of a test, I think, would feel more purposeful for the mental health counseling student.

Since I haven't taken the test, I don't feel qualified to recommend a particular study guide or program for you to use. I encourage you to look for yourself, and find the one that works best for you! But outside of official test prep resources, there are a lot of good recommendations for polishing your clinical skills that I *can* give you! Any of the *Practice Planners* series would be an excellent resource for practicing interventions by particular disorder. There is a *Practice Planners* book for practically every major problem and demographic group you can think of, so check them out. (Wiley) You also might try reading memoirs about people in therapy, or counselors in practice, taking into account their theoretical orientation's effect on their diagnostic choices. Some movies also provide great options for practicing picking out DSM-IV diagnoses. One of my favorite graduate classes was abnormal psychology, simply because the professor, Dr. Keith

Rosenbaum, made it so fun. We viewed different movies and then "argued" a diagnosis for the main character. I've included a short sampling of some movies that you could use to practice diagnostics in this way, but just search for "psychology and movies" and you'll find a ton of lists for any particular disorder. A word of caution though: a lot of these lists give away which diagnosis has been most often associated with that movie, so that takes some of the fun out of watching it. Also, sometimes they throw in disorder categories like "adolescence" which shouldn't really qualify as a DSM-IV pathology! Don't forget, whatever the internet may say about it, be careful to rely on the DSM-IV as the final word on the subject.

> DIAGNOSING THE
> MOVIES
> Identity
> One Hour Photo
> Donnie Darko
> The Manchurian
> Candidate
> Fight Club
> Lolita
> Girl, Interrupted
> As Good As It Gets
> Dexter (Series)
> A Beautiful Mind
> Matchstick Men
> Misery
> Momento
> The Other Sister

In many states, you are also required to take a Jurisprudence exam along with the major required test in order to apply for licensure. Jurisprudence refers to legal discipline and ideology of the law. It's a simple, no-fail test that took me 30 minutes, at most, to complete. The no-fail part is the best, of course. If taken online, the website does not allow completion of the test until you have answered the required number of questions correctly. A paper test is also designed to be repeated until the test-taker has passed, although it may take longer to correct any errors. Don't even bother sweating this. It's open-book, so just have a basic understanding of ethics and go for it.

Some states, such as Arkansas, Nevada, and Tennessee, require an oral examination along with a written one. I know, terrifying, right? But you can handle it. The oral exam in front of the state board tends to be scheduled after you've passed the written examination. Even states that don't require an oral examination for their professional counseling license *do* often have oral exams for school counselors and addiction counselors. Sometimes this can be done in lieu of a chunk of supervision hours.

It doesn't always stop there, either. In addition to the NCMCHE, to be licensed in Florida you must take an 8-hour laws and rules course, 2-hour prevention of medical errors course, and a 3-hour course on HIV/AIDS. Florida and other states also require specific courses be taken at the graduate level not generally required, like human sexuality. Arkansas requires license-seekers to present three letters of recommendation, two persons willing to attest to your training as a counselor, and a statement of intent. (I'm assuming "I intend to be a counselor" will not be sufficient.) Alabama residents also have to supply a Plan of Supervision, which is renewed yearly.

As you can see, it is not really possible to define universally what will be required to earn your license. This is why the ACA publishes a yearly report on state-by-state licensure requirements, available in their online bookstore. It's $29.95 for nonmembers, and $19.95 for members. Called *Licensure Requirements for Professional Counselors*, it's sure to be the simplest way to get the information needed. Find it by accessing the main page at counseling.org, clicking on the "Counselors" tab and bringing up the "Licensure & Certification" page. The link will be on that page.

If you like, you may also go directly to your state's counseling board site. Usually searching for "[state] counselor license" will be sufficient to locate the correct governing bodies.

APPLYING FOR LICENSURE

After you have decided on the license you wish to apply for (more about that in chapter six) and fulfilled the appropriate prerequisites (master's degree, testing, specific classes...) you can finally fill out the application for temporary licensure in your state. Each state has a board that governs counseling in their jurisdiction. Find that board's website and print out the form or forms they require. In addition to the actual application, you will almost definitely have to send in proof of passing test scores and a copy of a supervision agreement form. You can also use this opportunity to submit your practicum hours for consideration towards your total hours requirement. It is often the case that a certain amount of hours from your practicum courses (in which you saw clients or attended class) can actually count towards your overall total. Once you've mailed in everything that's requested (including the application fee) all that's left to do is sit back...and wait.

Remember when I told you about some dates earlier in this chapter, and I asked you to remember them? Here's why. I wanted you to see the timeline. I graduated May 15. I mailed off the application for the NCE with transcript and proof of degree a few days following that. Even if I hadn't been in Florida for the first week of June (the only week of testing in June in my area) when the email came through, they only offered me testing dates in July. Translation: It takes over two weeks to process a request for a test date. I tested on July 7, got my passing score and mailed it off by July 8. In the first week of August (nearly THREE MONTHS after graduation) I was officially licensed as a counselor intern. Technically, they approved me on July 27, and I was able to start counting hours on that day, but I didn't find that out until the approval came via snail mail in August. You may be able to get around that if your state provides the option to "Verify a Licensee" online. That's how I found out (on May 3, 2011) that I was officially licensed as an *independent* professional counselor. If you search for your name and it shows up online as a current intern licensee, you may start counting hours from that date that your license became official.

I had no idea when I started out how many steps were involved in applying for licensure. And in late April, when I started putting the application together, I nearly had a meltdown. I don't want you to have the same problem. It is a long process, and there's not really a way around it. Just plan on it and do what you have to do get through it. It's worth it in the end!

LIMITS OF LICENSURE

As a practicum counselor and then clinical intern, you have more freedom than ever before to practice counseling. However, the freedom is not unlimited.

In each stage, you must correctly disclose your status as a student or intern and get informed consent before providing services. You cannot practice unless your client knows you are an intern or practicum counselor and agrees *in writing* to accept your services. You cannot market yourself as a counselor unless you make it absolutely clear you are an intern under supervision. No ifs, ands or buts.

As an intern (I wouldn't even bother as a practicum student) you don't have the same opportunities to be an insurance provider as you do as a licensed counselor. Not that being a licensed counselor by any means guarantees you will be approved as a provider, but as an intern it's even more difficult. Not impossible, however. I was under the impression that no interns could apply for insurance panels while I was in the first year of my internship, but one day I happened to see intern providers in my area advertising that they were insured through a particular company, and I applied to that company. Much to my surprise, I was approved, even though I was still an intern counselor! Don't let you expectations get too high, but go ahead and check it out if you have the time. You never know!

Even if you are feeling pretty good about yourself getting approved on insurance panels and bringing in clients, you still cannot attempt to practice without supervision as a pre-licensed individual. I know, it sounds obvious, but there will be someone reading this going "really?" Really. Get an approved supervisor and work under them until your licensure as an independent practitioner is officially approved.

WHAT COUNTS? TRACKING HOURS

The questions I've heard indicate that there is a good deal of confusion related to what a new intern should do to document the hours they are spending under supervision. It is hard! In practicum, you have someone constantly following up on you, making sure that you are progressing at a decent pace to graduate. This time around, it's all you, baby.

It can be a little intimidating to take on this amount of record keeping all by yourself. After all, ultimately you will be accountable to the state board that this is an accurate portrayal of the time spent in internship. In my state, as I suspect is true for many others, there was no set form to mark off your hours on a regular basis. When the final application for licensure is submitted, you will be asked to disclose a total number, but it is not likely you will be required to turn in a detailed hour-by-hour record.

The exception to this rule is if you are audited. I hope this never happens, but if for some reason the board feels it is unlikely that you honestly earned these hours, they can request your records and verify down to the last hour whether you deserve credit for it or not. That's why I believe it is important for you to keep a record for yourself should they ever come knocking. You want to be able to verify that you honestly earned each precious hour.

There is no wrong way to keep track of this. I chose an Excel document, split into face-to-face hours and "other" hours, with notes for what the "other" hours might entail. (I might have been just a *little* paranoid.) I put in the numbers every day and added them up at the end of each month to see how many I'd accrued. This was handy also because I could look back and get an average of how many I typically earned in a month. Then I could start to guess how much longer it might take to reach the goal of licensure.

What counts as credited hours is not very well defined, so typically your supervisor should help you sort out what will and will not work. Just to get you started, here are some general rules of thumb:

- You don't get to count it as a counseling hour if the client doesn't show up.
- You *sometimes* get to count it as a counseling hour if it's on the phone.
- Notes, phone calls, work-related e-mails, professional research, conferences, professional association events, paperwork, case management and supervision sessions all count as "other."
- If you counsel at more than one location, *each location* must be submitted to the board for approval before you can start counting your hours there.
- Your supervisor should approve anything you're unsure about before you add it to your record.

PROFESSIONAL LIABILITY INSURANCE

You might think you can avoid professional liability insurance because you're "not going to do anything wrong." Sorry, even if you're the most ethical therapist of them all, you *must be covered by malpractice insurance at all times.*

First, because it is very unlikely you will be allowed to receive insurance payments from client's providers unless you are insured, and secondly you would be assuming a huge personal risk. Remember, you don't have to be guilty to be sued, and you still have to pay for legal fees even if you are not found liable for damages. You don't have to agree with me on that one because you don't have a choice in the matter!

To find an insurance provider that covers mental health care providers, search "mental health liability coverage," "mental health malpractice insurance," "counselor liability insurance," or some other combination of those buzzwords.

As a student in practicum, usually you are already insured through your school and the fee is covered by tuition. Before you start practicing as an intern, you must secure your own professional liability insurance. The coverage you are looking for in this case will likely be called "pre-licensed professional." If you cannot find a specific description that accurately describes your status, it would be better to call the insurance company and make sure that they cover interns. If you simply select "Professional Counselor" but don't check to make sure that the insurance provider includes interns under that umbrella, you may find out too late they won't cover your expenses.

Here are some of the things you might get coverage for as part of your package:

> *Carol's Comments:*
> Most of your clients will be rational, if troubled individuals. They want help sorting through their personal issues and that's why they've come to you. Some clients, however, are teetering on the brink. Malpractice insurance protects you and it is required by most agencies and hospitals. Get insurance.

- Legal fees related to appearing in court as a result of your professional actions.
- Within limits, disciplinary fees from the state board and civil investigation related to a problem with your counseling services.
- Medical expenses incurred as a result of your services.
- Expenses due to assault on your person or damage of your property.
- Reimbursement for loss of earnings resulting from a trial for an alleged malpractice.
- Reimbursement if you pay for first aid or medical fees in order to help someone who is in medical need as a result of your actions.
- Helpline or articles that will answer liability-related questions.
- Sometimes bodily injury occurring on business property, although if you are not the business owner, it is not likely this will apply to you.

Insurance policies cost money, but oftentimes there are discounts for students and new professionals, and additional discounts available to those who complete special training courses, work part-time, and much more.

BOTTOM LINE

Stressful? Yes. Complicated? Yes. Possible? Absolutely. You can do it.

CHAPTER FIVE
BEGINNING COUNSELOR MARKETING

WHY MARKET?

You may want to skip this chapter, thinking this is more for when you have your license and are opening your own business. I thought the same way, once. But soon enough I learned to think differently.

A major reason why you need to start opening up to the idea of marketing right now is that not every site will provide your clients for you. We covered this a little bit in the first and second chapters, but I will explain a little more about it here. The fact is, at some internship or practicum sites you will be expected to recruit clients on your own.

Sometimes, this can be a beneficial situation, if you are able to take a higher percentage of your client fees because you are doing more work to get them. The downside is that if you are not trained in marketing, you don't get any clients, or any hours. That is exactly what I want to help you avoid.

Even if your site does provide clients for you, more often than not they will not make up a full caseload. After all, you have to "compete" for these clients with the other interns in the office.

Carol's Comments:
If you want to increase your client load, appeal to a broader client base, get training in Play Therapy to see children, add to your education to enable you to do group work or create a specialty in divorce recovery or addiction issues. Listen to your own interests and add to your value as a therapist.

Whereas, if you market for yourself, the clients that respond to that marketing effort go only to you. No competition. So, even if you are supplied with clients, marketing will increase your existing client load. More than one way to get clients means more income, and more hours to help shorten the time it takes to qualify for your license.

Besides this, it's just good practice to start marketing as an intern. Think about it: if you try a marketing method that completely flops as an intern, the impact is significantly less. You don't have as much money or time invested now as you will when you have your own practice. Many interns want to open their own offices as soon as they qualify for licensure. What will they do if they end up "learning the hard way" then? When you're with an established group or organization, you have room to fail.

Marketing is good practice, it brings in clientele, and it also provides the counselor with a sense of personal value. After all, marketing is the first time you will get to start defining who you are as a professional. It is an opportunity to express the realization of your dreams. Marketing forces a normally self-effacing part of the population – counselors – to explore what they have to offer. Sometimes, we need something like that!

DEVELOPING YOUR PLATFORM

A platform: not just for Miss America anymore. These days, everybody has one. In this area, at least, I will encourage you to join the crowd.

A platform is a position statement. It's something you care about. You are an expert in your platform, or you are working on becoming an expert in your platform. It's a plan that is uniquely yours in regards to a specific issue and a specific population. It doesn't have to be your life goal, but as you develop your platform, you should realize that this is what you will become known for. For that reason, it needs to be something you like, and something you are comfortable being associated with for extended period of time.

Another way of looking at the word platform is as an elevator pitch: short and sweet, it characterizes that which makes other people *want what you have*. Let's look at some examples. Sandra Bullock is the *girl next door*. Mother Teresa *gave to others.* Platforms change based on the whims of the time to some degree, and different people (i.e. your clients) will be attracted to platforms for different reasons.

The simpler and more specific your platform is, the easier it will be for your clients to identify themselves with what you have to offer. Christina Katz, writer and platform guru extraordinaire, goes by the nickname *Writer Mama*. This tells people who are both writers and mothers that this person will have something interesting to say to them. Notice how she defined her platform by two key aspects: writers and moms. A good platform will have 2-4 key characteristics that make it specific and narrow enough that people who fit into the category will identify with.

> *Carol's Comments:*
> *Internship is a learning experience. Pay attention to yourself. Who do you enjoy working with, what group leaves you feeling really satisfied? Learn more about treating this demographic and you're on your way to a specialty.*

Think carefully about the audience you want to reach. The first question you need to ask yourself when developing your platform is "Who?" What's your demographic? Who is your ideal client? By this I mean what type of person are do you feel most comfortable with and/or most drawn to work with? What do they look like? This is not simply a question of physical type, such as age, gender, and ethnicity, but also of what makes up the marrow of this person? What do they care about? What are their struggles? What are their issues? I want you to go as deep down as you can.

Allow me to make an important side note: this is not about eliminating "undesirable" clients you don't wish to work with. As a counselor, we have an <u>ethical and moral</u> obligation to work with every client we are able to treat without bias. This exercise is instead about focusing on a group that will most benefit from what *you* have to offer.

I developed on answer to the "who" in my platform after I discovered how much I liked working with teenagers and young adults. Most of the time, you hear how teenagers are the least desirable group to work with. But in this case, I had the benefit of being a younger counselor. I was 23 when I started practicum. This was a group that I could work better with based on who I was at the time. I'm not their mom's age, so I'm not as much of a threat. I know that this advantage won't last forever, so I'm working with it while I can!

But your "who" may be more than one unique group of people. For example, I also know I can work well with Hispanic and East Indian ethnic groups despite the fact I'm Caucasian because I easily identify with and have experience with their cultures. Hispanic culture revolves around the family, and what others might see as "enmeshment" is perfectly normal for a nosy, interconnected Hispanic family. I was home-schooled – believe me, I know about close-knit families! I am also fascinated with the culture of India and have traveled in the country. The values, again, are very family-oriented. This is why I think these groups should be a part of my target demographic.

Your demographic may also, like mine, include members of a certain profession. There are a lot of high-stress fields out there that need good counselors. I happen to enjoy working with other counselors, particularly new counselors. It's fun to share in their joy of the work and encourage them through the nervousness everyone shares in the beginning. Why do you think I'm writing this book? I love talking to this group! So be sure to give some thought to what your ideal client does as a profession.

The next question to consider in developing your platform is "What?" What kind of licensure do you hold? How does that affect how you will do counseling?

Your type of licensure will affect the kinds of problems you will work with, the people you will see, and what you are allowed to do.

"When?" and "Where?" are questions that will also have to be answered in your advertisements, but are not really a part of your platform per se. Your address is likely to be a fixed location, and appointment times will vary. So I'm going to continue on past those question words and move on to "Why?" Now, this can be extrapolated into a big-picture question, so let me say at this point I'm only looking at "why" in reference to why these groups of people or "why" in the context of these particular problems. I will want to talk to you about "why counseling?" at a later point, but not now.

"How?" is the final question and the one your degree program most prepares you for. What's your theoretical orientation? What techniques do you believe in? Perhaps another way of stating the situation is "what is your modality?" But don't just stop at the technical description. What personal qualities make up your method of therapy? Are you particularly non-judgmental? An excellent listener? Giver of Unconditional Positive Regard? These are things the people want to know! You have something to offer. Share it!

How do you want to do counseling? Oh, sure, you may not have too much control over it now, but eventually you will and you want to start thinking about how to attract the person with "your" kind of problems. This statement can sound callous, like you're preying on a person with problems. The thing is, they're going to need help. And if you're good at it, it should be you that helps them. It's not taking advantage of them if you're an expert in your field.

How does doing counseling energize you? You probably already have a pretty clear idea of the answer to this question. It probably has a lot to do with why you went into counseling.

After answering these questions, your list may be very diverse. That's fine to start. But at the end of it all you need to shoot for a succinct, clear and unique platform that will draw others to you. Look it over objectively. Would you want to meet the person you're describing in your platform?

MARKETING PLAN

There is not one right way to make a marketing plan. I prefer the less formal approach – i.e. ideas scattered across a yellow legal pad. You might like having a five-page manifesto with bullet points and subheadings. Whatever floats your boat. Two things to be clear on, however, are budget and results.

Your budget, suffice to say, should not be more than the potential amount brought in by the new clients your plan attracts. There is a scale for this kind of thing: keep in mind plans that will work for right now and those that might be better suited for the future, when you're no longer an intern and (theoretically) bringing in more money.

Most interns should be able to afford a decent business card. These days you can get them practically free. Unless your sites are split, you probably want to get a card with your site's logo and address on it. Check with your supervisor or superior on-site and see if they have a preferred printing company, otherwise you should be able to take one of their cards in to any office supply store and have them scan the logo for you.

Outside of your name, address, telephone number and degree there are a ton of cool options you can add to your business card if you would like.

- Your slogan.
- Email addresses or websites.
- A place on the bottom or back of the card for clients to note appointment times.

- Special certifications.
- Theoretical orientation.
- Image(s).
- License number.

Play around with it until you get something you like. Make sure, however, that you are being specific about what your credentials are at all times. I know that will necessitate buying new business cards after you achieve full licensure, but you're going to have to deal with that. As we'll see soon in the section on marketing ethics, it is hugely important to make sure you are accurate in your advertisements.

If your site does not already have this covered, you might talk to them about increasing their web presence or getting a listing in the phone book. You can also discuss with them the possibility of putting up a short profile on your site's website with a picture to include as a part of their staff listings. Most counseling centers that offer intern services will have a mention of it on their website, but your referrals will increase exponentially if clients can request you by name.

> *Carol's Comments:*
> *As we've said before, check your state licensure requirements and the position on internship marketing. You'll almost always be required to list your intern status, but some states put restrictions on where and how counselors get to advertise.*

I also highly recommend pursuing a listing in *Psychology Today's* online Find a Therapist profile. You get a personalized listing, with profile picture, personal statement and a subscription to the magazine for about $30/month. Interested clients can contact you directly via phone or email, and your profile will be available on a multitude of sister sites. You can also select primary areas of expertise, insurance you offer (if any), range of fees, and more. Other potential listing services for therapists are

Goodtherapy.org, Therapy Tribe, Motivational Whisperers, and MyTherapistMatch.

If you have a little bit more disposable income, you can create a nifty website for yourself. However, it's probably best if you wait until your internship is over, and you are free to develop your own "brand" before you invest a lot of money in a fancy site of your own. In the meantime, there are many inexpensive or free website-hosting services that will allow you to begin to develop your professional identity.

The main thing to keep in mind is making yourself known, and you can be as creative in that as you want to be. Here are some ideas to get you started.

- Write a blog.
- Submit articles to local newspapers or relevant online sources.
- Leave your business card wherever you have an opportunity to do so. Many places of business have bulletin boards devoted to hosting other's business cards.
- Mail postcards or flyers with your info and a short pitch to people who might be interested in referring to you: local churches, schools, rehab centers that don't have private counselors on staff, and more.
- See about getting on a referral list at your place of worship.
- Start a group for free or low-cost, and use that to build your reputation and cultivate relationships with potential individual clients.
- Give lectures on counseling-related topics – your library, civic center or *alma mater* might let you do so under certain circumstances.

- Network. You may know a counselor who is great with eating disorders, which is not your specialty. Pass a few people on to this person that you wouldn't be able to take for yourself. Make sure the counselor knows you specialize in counseling for *fill in the blank,* and they may very well follow suit with clients they can't take.
- Volunteer. This builds a reputation for you in the community, and when people you've helped get asked about referrals to a good counseling service, guess who they're going to think of?

For more great ideas on counselor marketing, refer to David P. Diana's book, *Marketing for the Mental Health Professional* from John Wiley & Sons.

MARKETING ETHICS

Counselor marketing ethics are about more than just avoiding false advertising. Although a major portion of ethical counseling advertisement does revolve around accuracy, the other element that comes into play is the idea of *honor*. In this case, I use the word "honor" in the sense of keeping the best interests of others in your mind at all times. My understanding of both accuracy and honor is based in the ACA Code of Ethics, the code followed by most counselors along with their state code of ethics.

An ethical counselor makes sure that the information they use to advertise their services is as accurate as possible. They clearly delineate their *current* level of education and licensure. Even if you're a PhD candidate, you cannot advertise as a PhD until the degree is completely earned. (ACA Code of Ethics, C4b) Degrees must be categorized as earned or honorary. (C4c) You must not claim your program was accredited if it was not, and you can only claim accreditation if you went to the school *after* the accreditation was complete. (C4e)

When claiming membership to a professional organization, like the APA, ACA, AAMFT, and more, you must also be honest. (C4f) Are you a former member? If so, you can't advertise that you are a member, because that is misleading information. Any products or workshops you offer also must be presented honestly. (C3e) Don't advertise expertise you don't have, and don't make promises you can't keep, such as: "The *cure* for OCD!" "This book will save your marriage!" Tell the truth, and you will be fine.

Marketing counseling services requires a little extra care than marketing other services, because we are marketing to a vulnerable population. It's a significant responsibility. But it doesn't mean that counselors have to hide their talents from the outside world. Show what you have to offer, just do it with honesty and integrity.

CHAPTER SIX
CHOICES IN COUNSELING

D o you know where you want to end up? Whether you're a student starting an internship, just obtaining your license to practice, or somewhere in between, you will not all have the same goals. Some counselors will seek out the independence of private practice. Others will prefer the bustle and pace of a lively counseling agency. Many will seek dual licensure as a marriage and family therapist, or bypass their LPC altogether in favor of the systems-focused LMFT license. Those with a background in education may decide to shepherd young people as a school counselor. Numbers more will opt to sidestep these options to become licensed as a drug and alcohol counselor. What will you choose? It's all up to you!

AGENCY WORK

A significant percent of counselors will seek out careers at community mental health care agencies, correctional systems, parenting centers, family services, or any of the other worthy kinds of agencies that provide counseling services. These counselors may make an agency their first choice of places to work. Or, it may be the only option they have available. Regardless of why a counselor chooses agency practice, here are a few things they can come to expect from them.

Agencies use a hierarchical management structure. While private practice groups might be thought of as something of a democracy, agencies tend towards a chain of command. Each leader within an agency is responsible to someone else. The board of a nonprofit organization dictates policy to counselor supervisors, who in turn make sure their interns are in compliance with the rules. Government-run agencies, in a similar fashion, must answer to the requirements of the state. And everyone has to conform to the requirements of their insurance providers!

The agency setting's natural affinity towards structure often makes this a positive choice for counselor interns. Agencies are often very comfortable with using practicum students and interns, as they have established procedures in place to accommodate them. (Good for both parties, as interns can easily slip in and out of the system as need be.) Sometimes agency internships are hard to obtain if all their available spots are taken, but conversely, agencies usually look to fill a spot as soon as one opens up.

Agencies are nearly always busy, which is great news for those of you seeking counseling hours. It is why, in my opinion, even interns who eventually want to become private practitioners often start out in an agency. You can't beat this advantage in logging required hours! In some private practices, you can easily limp along for years trying to get your required face-to-face time. In an agency setting, both face-to-face hours and "other" hours are quickly accomplished due to the demands of paperwork and meetings. That is why it's extremely unlikely you will struggle with completing your internship on time at an agency. On the flip side, with a higher workload level, you will <u>have</u> to be extra-careful to practice good self-care or risk burnout.

Agencies provide you with one of the largest and most diverse network of counselors, social workers, and caseworkers to learn from and befriend! Private practice can be a little lonely at time, if your group doesn't have a good way of staying connected. In an agency, you will work closely with people in many different kinds of helping careers. This is also good for clients, because it allows them access to a more integrated care network.

> Carol's Comments
>
> There are good reasons why "self-care" has become a buzzword in our profession. You may love hearing about and helping with others' problems, but you need a disconnect to help from being bogged down. Find a physical outlet. Learn the way you like to play. You're building a career, but you need to take steps to prevent burnout.

In case you don't already know, integrated care is generally considered the best method of care delivery for the client. The idea is to work in conjunction with other helping professionals and use all available resources to help the client. In private practice, you can get into a rut of referring clients to psychiatrists, social service agencies, career counselors, and self-help groups even when you have little to no relationship with the providers of these services. This is pretty unethical and a compromise of care.

Clients aren't always able to successfully plot a course through all the various different kinds of providers on their own. Navigating the network of insurance providers, social service agencies, housing services, the legal system, and so on is not an easy process. It's hard enough for us, as people who work within the system itself, to deal with it all! How can we expect our clients to handle it, when they haven't worked with the system before and at the same time are wrestling with mental health challenges? Integration of care lessens the chance that a client will slip through the cracks – and that's a cause worth fighting for.

The pay at an agency is generally not substantial, but there are opportunities for advancement. Once you've worked at one agency, there's a little bit of an "in-crowd" feeling when you apply to another one. For example, should you need to relocate, it is a lot easier to transfer to another, similar agency.

Because at an agency, almost anyone can qualify for counseling aid and there are never enough resources to go around, you might sometimes feel helpless as an agency counselor to meet this great need. It can be overwhelming trying to focus on one person, knowing there are ten more on a waiting list who need your help just as badly!

But you're in a valuable and unique position to reach out to some people who've experienced the worst life has to throw at them and survived. They will inspire you with their endurance, and you will inspire them with your faith in them. In fact, YOUR belief in them might be the only thing that can help them turn their life around. It's an incredible privilege to be in that position.

MARRIAGE AND FAMILY THERAPY LICENSURE

Earning a MFT license is similar to and can overlap with LPC training. Depending on whom you speak with, it can be considered more prestigious, equal to, or less prestigious than general counseling licensure. Up until recently, it was the only kind of counselor that existed in the state of California.

MFTs will deal with pretty much the same problems as LPCs, but they are trained to deal with problems in the framework of the family. Standard counseling practice treats the individual. MFTs also recognize an individual, but their perspective is rooted in the context of the family. The areas they will study are slightly different, also. In "therapy-speak," rather than spending time concentrating on Bowen or Adler, the student of marriage and family therapy will focus on Satir, Minuchin and Salvador.

If you love family counseling theories, you will love the marriage and family degree. You will have the opportunity to learn great techniques to help family groups. But even if you don't get your *degree* in marriage and family therapy, you can often still obtain an MFT license. You will usually have to take additional classes not included in the basic counseling master's, but often this is not over-burdensome to do. You will still have to undergo supervision and apply for licensure as a marriage and family therapist, as you did for your counselor license. However, if you start your licensure tracks <u>at the same time</u>, you can count counseling hours that overlap towards BOTH licenses. So if you know you will want to do both licensures, do them at the same time. It will save you a headache!

So how do you know whether you want to do one, both, or neither?

Let me start with the principle that training is good. We never want to skimp on quality of care when it comes to our clients. But, most of us don't have a lot of cash to throw around, and extra school takes away from family time and the ability to work at your primary job. That's why it is important to be thoughtful in making this decision. When you are considering whether or not to pursue any kind additional training, ask yourself first if you need the license or certification to do the job you want to do.

Then, what do you consider to be your primary goal in counseling? If it's working with couples and families, then it's probably worth it to get your MFT degree and LMFT license. You will get a better education in those areas. However, not achieving this license doesn't mean you can't ever see couples or families. Licensed counselors can still do that! It's just not their primary area of expertise. If you don't think at the moment that you would want to work chiefly with couples and families, I would wait and find out more about it before doing the extra work.

SCHOOL COUNSELING

To work in school counseling requires that the prospective counselor take specific graduate courses in guidance counseling. It also is necessary that the counselor have some level of teaching experience before working as a school counselor. The specifics of this experience will vary. Some states require a master's in school counseling, others two years of teaching experience, some teaching certification, and so on. If you want answers related to your specific state, I would suggest you visit the American School Counselor Association at schoolcounselor.org.

School counselor certification is not something you can just pick up casually along with your LPC/LPCC. If you want to be a school counselor, you should either start on the track early or plan on taking time to reach your goal. Many school counselors start out as teachers who decided later on to pursue the extra courses to be certified as a school counselor as well.

Like other jobs involving the school system, as a school counselor you would probably be out of work over the summer, which is not necessarily a bad thing. You will likely be required to come in early to school and stay late in many cases in order to meet with parents. Academic guidance, mediating disputes, and dealing with issues like drugs, teen pregnancy, and eating disorders are some of the many responsibilities you will be taking on. Other responsibilities of school counselors can include producing regular seminars, assemblies and resources on health issues, such as dating violence. Many school counselors will also be expected to take charge of student emotional health after a major disaster, like a tornado or a school shooting.

Maintaining client privacy in the school system can be more difficult than in a private practice setting, as some of my teenaged clients have confirmed. Even if you are the soul of discretion, there may be cases in which other teachers, administrators, or even parents unthinkingly spread a secret from your files. This can result in some of your students feeling distrustful of you.

If what I've described above sounds exciting and fulfilling, then school counseling is probably the job for you! Check out the ASCA and find out what you need to do to get started in the field.

SUBSTANCE ABUSE COUNSELING

Acquiring a license to be a drug and alcohol counselor is a similar process to being licensed as a professional counselor, the major difference being that a person doesn't always have to have a master's degree to qualify. In some cases a bachelor's degree is sufficient when combined with specific drug and alcohol counseling classes, supervised experience, and a written and oral exam.

Counseling for addiction differs from traditional counseling in that it focuses more on assessment, treatment planning and working in group settings. LADCs (also known as LACs, Licensed Addiction Counselors) will need to be prepared for emergency/crisis intervention and understand the biological as well as psychological process of addiction.

COUNSELING THROUGH SOCIAL WORK

Just as not all counselors will end up in the same place, not all will come from the same place, either. It is common for many counselors these days to come from a background in social work. In fact, some people will argue that it's actually better to have the social work degree than the counseling degree! There's a significant movement right now that purports the smartest choice when planning a counseling career is to pursue a social work degree first. It *is* perfectly legitimate for social workers to provide counseling services in many cases. As part of their program, social workers can choose to specialize in the study of counseling. If they do so, they receive a shorter version of the training available in traditional counseling programs.

What proponents of MSW (Master's in Social Work) counselors most of often cite as the chief benefit of this degree is "hire-ability." Agencies may be more likely to be seeking out and hiring LCSWs (Licensed Clinical Social Workers) rather than LPCs. However, there are also twice as many LCSWs as there are LPCs, so it's hard to tell whether their jobs are more in demand or they're simply more recognizable.

Even if there are more jobs available for MSWs, it doesn't necessarily mean you should immediately transition to a master's degree in social work. For one thing, the perception of counselors' work seems to be improving in the wider community. Sanctions against using LPCs in the military and in VA hospitals have recently been relaxed. This tells me that just because something is the way it is now, doesn't mean it is the way it will always be!

Additionally, while you will probably have more job opportunities if you have a degree in social work, you also have to consider that they may not be the job opportunities that you want! What use is a certain kind of degree if it helps you do something you don't want to do? If you don't enjoy studying the MSW coursework as much as you would a MA/MS in Counseling Psychology, then go with the counseling degree. If you won't appreciate the material, you shouldn't invest in the degree.

Another factor increasing the level of appreciation other people have for them is that MSWs have historically had tougher programs. But the widening umbrella of CACREP-accreditation is changing that. Accreditation by CACREP, which is specifically for universities that offer counseling degrees, offers graduates a higher level of respect from potential employers. If you graduated from a CACREP-accredited school, in many cases your counseling degree will be considered as distinguished as a MSW.

The MSW counselors I know have expressed both sides of the situation. On the one hand, many of them value the extended range of options the degree provided them. Others begrudge the extra casework and paperwork that can come when being hired as a MSW counselor. Despite the

> *Carol's Comments*
> There is quite a bit of over-lap in these areas of counseling, although the licensures can be different. School Counselors frequently deal with substance-addicted youth and even parents with substance issues. Social Work counselors often deal with individual's personal issues. The areas of training concentration may be different, but in reality counselors deal with individuals and families who may have multiple issues.

differences in final destination, I have seen no significant difference as far as knowledge and ability between the licensed social work counselors and the licensed professional counselors. Education and skill depend largely on the person. Counselors must be motivated to grow and challenge themselves at their job because of something inside them, not because of their degree.

In conclusion, if you're divided on which area of the helping profession you'd like to end up in, definitely, go the social work route. If your primary concern is finding agency employment, again, social work *may* be your best bet. However, if you know you want to be a counselor and nothing else, you might as well pursue the entire counseling curriculum to get the fuller education.

CHAPTER SEVEN
A DAY IN THE LIFE OF A BEGINNING COUNSELOR

APPOINTMENTS

$\bigwedge$aking and keeping appointments will be the center of your world as an emerging new counselor. Yet, how do you, as a beginning counselor, first obtain clients to make appointments with? If, as was discussed in the previous chapter, you work in an agency, you may have clients showing up for you all day long. You may never have the opportunity to make an appointment for yourself, because a client is always there, in need! But most of the time, even in agencies, at some point or another you will have to make an appointment.

As a beginning counselor, your supervisor or your office manager may handle most of the initial client contact or you might end up making the first contact directly. Another possibility is that you will give your supervisor your available times and trust that they will fill your spots on your behalf.

Making client appointments sounds simple, but it can get complicated in no time. There is always a continual fight for the most-desired time slots; evenings, weekends and after-school times go first. If your future or present practice involves seeing a lot of children, you may fill up in the late afternoon and evening and be empty throughout the rest of the day. That means that you might consider marketing to some different kinds of clients to fill your available spots. The next two groupings of popular appointment times are early morning slots (these usually appeal to moms who have just dropped their kids off at school) following by lunchtime appointments, which are the best time for many 9-to-5 employees.

I bring this up so that early on in your planning, you can decide for yourself how many of these time slots you are willing to make available. It really isn't a good idea to put off a decision about this. If you don't make a firm boundary related to your availability, your clients will eventually take up <u>all</u> your time. This is the perfect recipe for early burnout. We don't want that! So in order to avoid this trap, envision what YOU choose your counseling experience to look like! What did you come up with?

PAYMENT OPTIONS

In the chapter "Boundaries in the Therapeutic Relationship," payment concerns in terms of the therapist's attitudes about money and the potential effect of money on their relationships with clients will be discussed. But for now, we're just going to focus on the mechanics of collecting payments in your office.

How do you get paid? (If you don't receive fees directly, how does your site get paid for your work?) What will be your role in dealing with the financial side of things? Will you collect the fees? Will you be responsible for updating clients on their bill? Are you going to be using collectors for unpaid debt?

> **Carol's Comments**
> There are significant reasons why 'self-care' is important to counselors. You need to protect and nurture <u>you</u>. When clients step into your office, they deserve the best counselor. You deserve to be the best counselor. With this in mind, make a schedule that allows you to feel and function at the top of your game.

You may not have a lot of choice in the money matters at first. Or, you may have much more responsibility than you want! Some sites are so small that they can't afford a receptionist. In that case, you will need to get comfortable with addressing the money issue head-on. But even if you don't personally collect money, you will still need to be prepared for the inevitable issues that come with it!

When I got started in counseling, I thought it would always be therapeutically advantageous to have a receptionist collect the fees. I believed that I could remain a neutral party in the financial arena that way. But that doesn't actually work out as well as it sounds. In my case, we had a receptionist, but clients still brought up the money issue with me. I had to bring it up with them, too. As I based my fees on a sliding scale, I had to discuss sensitive issues like income, debt, alimony and child support on a regular basis. It ended up that I was regularly hearing about difficult money situations and still had to ask a client to pay a fee afterwards.

Are you comfortable with asking for a fee you deserve, even if your client doesn't have a great deal of income? Or, beyond that, can you handle it if a client hears your fee and starts trying to bargain you down? This does happen, especially if you're offering a sliding scale. Your first instinct in this situation may be to buckle, worrying about the impact on the client's emotional health. While it is important to consider the client's emotional health, it doesn't necessarily mean that it's your responsibility to cave in to whatever they demand.

What will help a generally touchy situation the most is that you know for yourself why you set the fees that you did. Even if you did not structure the fees yourself, you can find out what criteria your place of work used to set their

> *Carol's Comments*
> Remember that most people, no matter what income they have, feel strapped. They typically want to spend the least amount. Don't take this personally or let their money concerns convince you that you're not worth the fee you need to charge. You need to pay your electric bill and you deserve a vacation now and then.

rates. Usually sliding scale fees have a minimum, so you could choose to start there. Why did you or your site choose that minimum? Because that's what you (or your site) needed you to earn in order to keep working there. That is a valid reason.

Ours is a fee-for-service industry. Criteria that are perfectly acceptable to consider when setting fees include industry standards and overhead expenses. Also, it is okay to base your fee on the answer to the question of how many other people are able to do what you do. Use these reasons when explaining your fees and it will feel less personal to the client. This way you can avoid it having too much of a negative impact on the therapeutic relationship.

TAKING NOTES

Notes can function in a multitude of ways. They can be used as notes to self or can read like an essay on the themes of the session. Your observations may be a line-by-line description of what happened in session. (Then he said, then I asked, then he responded...) Your notes could also simply be a recording of events: nothing more, nothing less!

SOAP Notes are a common note-taking format used by therapists and other medical professionals. They are comprised of four major elements, indicated by the acronym "SOAP." S stands for subjective, O for Objective, A for Assessment, and P for Plan. Though you certainly don't have to use the SOAP note format, it's a common enough format that you should know the basics of how it works.

The first area, Subjective, refers to the client's personal feelings about their situation, or each member of a couple's individual accounts of recent events. On the other hand, Objective concerns are able to be measured and observed. If the client comes in smelling like pot, or scores a certain way on the MMPI-2, these would be objective aspects to record on your notes. Assessment is your diagnosis of the client. For you, this would be a DSM-IV diagnosis and, on succeeding notes, further observations that either enhance or detract from the diagnosis. Your Plan is what you're planning on doing about it. What interventions do you have up your sleeve? What other remedies might the client be trying on his or her own? (Perhaps journaling, or a medication regimen?)

You do not have to use any established formula for creating your notes, SOAP or otherwise, unless your site requires you to. You could just as easily create a unique template that works for you and use it over and over again. You should, however, always include in your notes the date the person was seen, any interventions that were used, and identify which client the note refers to by either a name or a number. Notes that are mechanically produced (typed) must be initialed to indicate the identity of the person who wrote the note.

Some big no-no's when taking notes: Don't write opinions or personal feelings about the client. First, they are legally allowed to read their own notes, so they could eventually see what you wrote about them. Secondly, it's not something that's helpful to you. You're supposed to be providing them with proper care no matter what your personal feelings about them may be. Writing about them negatively in your notes will just reinforce your problems with the client every time you re-read your client file. So don't do it!

> *Carol's Comments*
>
> You are ethically and legally required to keep notes. This is part of the job, but it's up to you to find the method that works best and is least burdensome for you.

Another big mistake you can make with your notes is not writing them. I know you're tired at the end of a long day and it seems unbearable to produce one more note at that time. But try to not let more than a day go by between the time of your session and writing your notes about it. Your memory will fade and you will risk losing significant aspects of situations that you could have followed up on later. Also, you can get yourself in a situation where it's the end of a semester and your practicum supervisor won't approve your hours until you catch up on the 30 notes you've been putting off! Nightmare. Avoid this situation at all costs.

In addition to the do-it-yourself option, there's note-taking software available. TherapyNotes.com, TheraManager, Epitomax, Confidant and AppointmentsPRO are some notable providers of this kind of service. Some are a flat fee and others (TherapyNotes) are billed on a monthly basis. You may benefit from these, but they are probably cost-prohibitive until you really get your practice going. Use your own judgment.

Really, the purpose of note taking is just to have something to help you remember what you have been developing session-to-session and to allow another therapist to take over your work smoothly if they needed to. As long as your notes accomplish that goal successfully, you are probably going to be fine.

PHONE CALLS

Though for most people, your main client contact will be in person, you will also spend a great deal of time setting up appointments and checking in over the phone.

When you're looking at phone calls, know your own personal boundaries. What I mean by that is know what you're comfortable discussing over the phone. Some subjects you may want to save for in-session, because they're too personal, or you're not sure of the client's security or privacy, or simply because it isn't the appropriate time to talk about it.

A lot of clients would like it if we were available whenever they needed us to be, by phone, email, or in-person! In an ideal world, that would be wonderful. But in our world, that's not possible. If we were constantly on-call we would end up potentially neglecting other clients, creating dependency, and compromising our own self-care. So if you're not primarily a phone counselor, I would seriously consider placing boundaries on how often your phone conversations last more than ten minutes.

I know it's hard to cut someone short on the phone, and I suggest you do it very gently. But do it. Scheduling appointment times creates a set of lessons for the client that is too helpful to compromise. Regular sessions teach our clients that there is a time and a place to deal with problems. It also gives them power, because it indicates we trust them to take care of themselves between sessions. Therapy is more than what happens in a session, it is also comprised of modeling a healthy lifestyle and treating our clients like the responsible, functional adults we are grooming them to be.

Phone sessions, however, are a different story. Phone sessions that are scheduled can be extremely helpful if a client doesn't have time to drive over on their lunch break, but could still talk to you on their cell phone in the car. Phone sessions are also often a great last-minute substitute in a client emergency. I once engaged in a phone session with a parent of a teen I was seeing because she locked her keys in the car on the way to come see me! It would have been over an hour before someone could come rescue her, so since we were both planning on using this time anyway, we just "met" on the phone instead.

The other thing that consistently comes up in regards to phone etiquette is leaving messages. It's a common enough thing: here comes the beep, you know what to do. But in a counseling relationship, you have to consider a person's privacy. What if your client lives with a roommate? Even worse, what if they live with an abusive partner, and are attending counseling in secret? Unless you have absolute permission (by that I mean a signed release) to leave detailed information on a person's voicemail, don't do it! You can't risk getting them into danger, or embarrassing them. The choice to attend counseling is a private one, and should remain that way.

CONFIDENTIALITY

Confidentiality. Ugh. It seems so simple in graduate school. (Those were the good old days.) Just don't talk about what happens in session. No problem, right?

In reality, it's about as easy to put into practice as playing piano with both hands tied behind your back. First of all, *confidentiality* is different than *privacy*. Privacy is a human right to have one's secrets protected. It's the building block of trust that forms the counseling relationship, but it doesn't hold up in court. Confidentiality is a legal right. It is what we can be sued for breaking.

This can be completely nerve-wracking for the beginning counselor. It seems so easy when we're discussing it in school. Then we start counseling, and the parent of a teenager we're seeing approaches us while our client slips out to the car. Or we have to give a diagnosis so that our clients can qualify for Employee Assistance Program aid. Maybe we have to record our client sessions for supervision.

That's when it gets a lot more complicated.

As was addressed in the first chapter, often consent forms for interns contain a notification that sometimes interns will have to record the client's sessions, either by video or audio. Again, even if this is the case, you should clear it with them on the day of and make sure they're comfortable with it. Also, the tapes should never be shared with anyone outside of your supervision group or your practicum class. To do so definitively breaches confidentiality.

You now know that when you are leaving a phone message that you need signed permission to go into any detail. However, if someone calls your office and asks you straight out, "Is so-and-so a client of yours?" don't hesitate. Your standard line is "I can neither confirm nor deny that I am seeing this person for counseling." Repeat this as often as is necessary. This also applies for anyone who asks you this question in person, but in this case be extra careful that your expression doesn't give you away! Really, graduate schools should have to teach counselors how to keep poker faces as a standard aspect of the program. We are so often asked awkward or potentially complicated questions!

Use caution. People can be sneaky when they really want this kind of information. Parents of teenagers can feel entitled to know about what their adolescent discloses, but even parents of adult children will sometimes feel that they have a right to know about what you discuss in session, because they're paying for it.

Remember this: because an individual – any individual - is paying for counseling DOES NOT MEAN they have a right to know what is said in counseling. No one is forcing them to pay for it. If they don't like it, they have the right to stop paying, but they still don't get to know! You'd be surprised how often I've heard "but I'm paying for it" as an argument. I don't care! I'm still not breaking my client's confidentiality.

Unfortunately, this is only true of an individual paying for another individual's counseling sessions. I wish it could be true for EAPs (Employee Assistance Programs) and insurance providers as well, but often it isn't. It may be a little while before you have any dealings with insurance companies, since they rarely take on interns, but you need to be prepared. For some insurance companies and EAPs, you have to provide a suggested treatment plan, a diagnosis, and perhaps even some explanation of interventions used. This feels strongly like it breaches confidentiality, but it actually doesn't.

If the client has authorized it, we don't have any choice in the matter but to reveal with the insurance provider requests. It can be frustrating when not only do we compromise privacy by working with managed care, but we also invite them into the treatment process. While insurance professionals are probably quite competent in their field, they know almost nothing about ours. Yet they are allowed to tell us how many sessions we get with a client, and whether our diagnosis is "acceptable" or not.

This is why many counselors choose not to work with managed care. You may perhaps make this choice as well. But if you do not, you will be not only asked to release privileged information, but expected to as well. Clients, however, do expect this, and usually are not squeamish about signing release forms for you to communicate with their managed care provider. While it would be thoughtful of you to warn them of possible ramifications of disclosing a diagnosis and suggest private pay if at all possible, in the end, it's up to the client.

Another important confidentiality conflict arises when you run into your client outside of the office. It's a situation I never actually thought about before I started working as a counselor, but it is a major potential confidentiality breach. Think about it. If you see your client in public, chances are one of you isn't alone. If you come over and introduce yourself as their counselor, you've just spilled the beans that this person is in counseling, either to their companion or yours. Awkward. And illegal.

However, you don't want your client to think you don't care about them. That's why I copied a sign Carol has up in her office, that says she doesn't acknowledge clients she sees outside of the office. She also states that if *they* want to talk to her, she will be happy to do so. Posting a sign like this makes sure that her clients know that she isn't ignoring them, but preserving their privacy. Most clients will not have considered this and be grateful that you have. The ones who don't care will go ahead and talk to you in public, and that's fine. If they "out" themselves, there's no breach of confidentiality.

There's also no breach of confidentiality if a client is discussed within a group or agency itself...usually. It would be very hard to do business without within-agency confidentiality! The office manager needs to know some information to deal with the paperwork or insurance claims, although most office managers make it a point of pride not to peek in client session notes. To be clear, I think that that it should be stated on the informed consent that confidentiality is within the entire agency or group.

Within the same office, you will also have to discuss cases on occasion with other counselors to determine appropriate standards of care for a particular disorder or dysfunction. This is part of being a good counselor, and usually okay if you're careful not to take the information outside the office and you make it a point to thoroughly disguise the identifying details.

Each state has its' own legal nuances of the confidentiality clause. In Texas, a judge can waive confidentiality with you on the stand. Then, you will have answer whatever question they ask of you. And then there are the lawyers. With lawyers come subpoenas, which include not only the summons to appear in court, but also a subpoena for your notes at times. When you get a subpoena, you have to do what it says or risk being in contempt of court. But there's a difference between an official subpoena, (coming from the legal system) and a request for information. A request for a copy of your notes can come from a government agency, a client's employer or school, or the client themselves. You can decline a request (and in fact you should) if a client has not authorized you in writing to release your notes to the agency.

YOUR OFFICE

Your own office! Excitement swells just hearing those words. It was a thrill for me too, the first time I worked in my own office, and even before then, when I shared several rooms with a few interns in my group. Whether your work environment is communal or all on your own, here are a few things you might consider in planning the layout of your first office.

First, it's important that the room in which you conduct sessions be comfortable and inviting. No, you don't have to go buy a fainting couch, but it would be nice if you did your best to pull in the comfiest chairs and a few extra pillows if you can snare them. Think about where you will sit, and where they client will sit. This can be a flexible concept, but I must say having a chair that was "mine" helped me subconsciously slip into counselor mode whenever I sat in it. I also set up a two clocks in my line of vision, one behind one client chair, and one behind the other. That way no matter which client I was looking at I could keep track of my timetable so my client didn't have to. It's easier to keep up with time unobtrusively if you're used to the location of your timepieces.

I would remove any physical barriers between you and your client before you start counseling. Even a coffee table, psychologically, can feel like a wall. Side tables, though, beside the clients or the counselor can be helpful, as clients often bring in their cup of coffee or can of soda into session. Side tables are also useful for holding Kleenex boxes, as clients need to have access to these at all times.

Choosing proper lighting is another part of your first office setup. If you have only bright overhead florescent lighting, it might be worthwhile to put in a strong lamp behind the client or behind you, to have a softer option. However, you don't want to have the room too dark, or else you risk your client falling asleep! Unless you're a hypnotherapist, this probably isn't a great idea. I suggest creating two lighting methods, one quite bright and one dim but not dark.

You should have some room to move around in your office. Women will bring in large purses with them that take up big chunks of your floor space, and expressive types may wave their arms around or even get up while they talk to you. Also, if you work with kids a lot, you will want to be able to sit on the floor with them or move the tables between you (this is the exception to the barrier rule!) to share crayons, paper and markers.

You may want to bring extra chairs in and out for groups, and you may want to have your own desk to work on client notes and papers in between sessions. I highly recommend having your own desk if you can swing it, because whenever I would go into the main office at the Family Counseling Center to write my notes, I would always ended up chatting with Debbie, the office manager, instead! I blame her...if she wasn't fun to talk to I wouldn't have had a problem with that. But that's why I needed my own desk. I wouldn't get any work done otherwise.

I recommend also having two trashcans, one behind your desk to hold trash from your paperwork and one near your client's chair for Kleenex or drinks. It's uncomfortable for a client to have to hold a bunch of wadded-up Kleenexes in their hands for the whole session. If you don't want your clients to throw away drinks in your office trashcans for fear of attracting insects, be prepared to show them to the appropriate trash can instead. Be careful not to leave anything that can identify client information in either trash. You should always shred it if you can or file it in a separate, locked room.

Speaking of files, make sure you follow appropriate guidelines for storing privileged information at all times. I would keep all files in a central location if you're working with a group or agency. Limit the personal information you keep in your possession, and don't take client files home. Your home is not secure, and your roommate, spouse or children shouldn't accidentally see any of the names on your files. What if they happened to know one of these people?

Also, use caution when transporting files as well...I heard a story of a counselor changing offices who carried his files in the trunk of his car, and then got into an accident. His clients' private information scattered all over the freeway. There was a one in a million chance something like this could occur, but it did. He had to call his clients and disclose to them that their privacy was compromised, even though he couldn't have seen this coming. Bet that was an awkward conversation!

You cannot prevent a freak accident like this, but you can reduce your liability. If you can demonstrate that you use extreme care on a regular basis, it is less likely you would be liable for any random breach like the car accident that happened to the counselor above.

CORE COMPETENCE TWO: CLIENT RELATIONSHIPS

CHAPTER EIGHT
THE FIRST SESSION

No matter how excited you are to start this job, no matter how great your site, the first session represents a major change in the game. Prior to this moment, you have dealt in theory, now you're crossing the line into practice. So what happens next?

HOW DO I START THE SESSION?

Your name! People will want to know who you are. You might also want to include your title: student counselor, counselor intern, MFT intern, or something else along those lines. Many new counselors will feel the obligation to disclose their credentials – or lack thereof – immediately, but the student or intern is likely the only one worried about this. As an intern or practicum counselor, you have the backing of your site to prove your competency. That's usually enough for most clients.

After you've taken a seat across from your new client for the first time, they will be unsure of where to start. You might be too, but it's your job to be the leader here. In time, you'll probably settle into your own unique opener, but while you're still developing your style, here's a few ways you might choose to start:

The Classic:

What brings you in here today?

The Intake Cheat:

I see from your intake form that you're experiencing miscommunication in your relationship. Would you like to tell me a little bit more about it?

The Observation:

I see you're looking a bit concerned. Would you like to ask me any questions before we start?

The Big Picture:

So what's your story?

The Icebreaker:

So this is a little bit weird, talking about personal things with a stranger. Do you have any questions for me about how this works?

The Theory:

I'm a(n) _____ therapist (Adlerian, Gestalt, etc.) This means I believe healing happens through_____. So today I'm going to start by _____.

Beyond these few ideas, the possibilities are literally limitless. Try a few on for size until you find one that feels comfortable for you.

> *Carol's Comments:*
> *Unless clients specifically request a kind of therapy or a theoretical orientation (most don't), they probably won't have interest in this. They're troubled by something in their lives or they wouldn't be there.*

HAVING CONFIDENCE

You might be trying your best in this first session to project an air of calm, but if you're feeling anything like I was my first time counseling, you are completely terrified. Before my first session I had this horrible, recurring thought, "What if I completely mess them up?" Looking back, it's hard to believe I was ever that scared. But most of us are. It's a serious task we're taking on! But I have to tell you, if this is what you're feeling, your non-verbals are going to give you away. As hard as it is, you have to shut off the possibility of failure in this first session, for the sake of your client. It is there. It will always be there. But consider another side to it. How much responsibility for how the session turns out should you really take on yourself?

> *Carol's Comments:*
> *Remember you do have a lot to offer clients. If you do nothing but really listen and understand their problems, you'll be giving them a lot. Some clients say they want specific answers to questions you cannot possibly answer for them. Don't get sucked into this. Just offer yourself and your honest (considered) suggestions. Clients really need to find their own best answers.*

You <u>are</u> the leader, and it <u>is</u> your responsibility to manage the client and give them the best possible treatment you have to offer at the time. But you cannot control what they do with it. That's up to them. You can't make them get better. That's their choice. You can only facilitate their improvement.

Your confidence should come from inside. It should come from the fact that you've had more education than they have in this particular subject. I'm not saying you are superior to them. But this is your area. It's like if you were taking your car into the mechanic's. The mechanic is an expert in cars. In the counseling office, you are the expert in counseling. While you cannot know everything about their life and what will always work for them, you have the knowledge of where to start.

If you don't know all the things they need you to know right away, that's fine! You have *access* to the knowledge they need, through your supervisor, your school, and the latest counseling research. If you don't know what to say the day of the session, tell them that. It's fine to say to your client, "I'm not sure about that right now. Let me think on that and get back to you." This gives you time to do some research, or to wait for inspiration to strike. I believe that it gives you more credibility with clients that you are willing to devote time to coming up with the best response, rather necessarily always having the right answer off the top of your head.

Draw your confidence, too, from your desire to help others. Don't underestimate how much credibility that gives you. With that desire comes motivation, and with motivation comes change. If you truly desire to help others, you are going to work hard at making that happen. Determination produces right results more often than not, which is something that should also inspire your confidence in yourself!

SELF-DISCLOSURE

There are two kinds of self-disclosure I want to talk about here: inappropriate self-disclosure and professional disclosure. One is good, and one not so good. Want to guess which is which?

Inappropriate self-disclosure might happen when we're nervous, when we're not emotionally healthy or when we're angry. For example, if you as the counselor don't know what to say, you may end up talking too much about yourself. This is normal at the beginning, but please try to remember that this is the client's session, not yours. When you're paying them a hundred bucks an hour, you get to talk about you. Since they're paying you, THEY get to be the center of attention. Nervous self-disclosure tends to taper off as you get more and more comfortable being in the therapist's chair.

Emotionally unhealthy self-disclosure emerges when a counselor has gotten into the profession for the wrong reason. Listen, it's an open secret that we're all a little crazy. Why else would we do this job? I've had my own problems, and I expect to have more in the future. But you can't do counseling in order to fix that in yourself. You have to do counseling to help others.

If you recognize yourself in the above paragraph, put this book down and call your own therapist. If you don't have one, get one. Many schools now are requiring counseling students to get counseling themselves. I think that is a very appropriate decision. We all have "stuff," and the sooner we deal with it the better.

Inappropriate self-disclosure also sometimes comes out when you're angry. Listen, I'm going to get personal here. My future mother-in-law passed away during my practicum. I did take some time off, and I did request that my supervisor steer clients dealing with grief to another counselor for a time. But there were times even talking to ordinary clients when I would get a sudden urge to shake them, and say, "Get over it. My children won't know their grandmother. I have it worse than you do."

Of course, that was grief disguised as anger. And no, I never said anything out loud. But I could have. And if I did, that would have definitely been inappropriate self-disclosure. Their problems weren't less significant than mine. They were just different.

As counselors, we have to constantly monitor our own emotions and motivations to make sure that we're on the right path. It's our responsibility to our clients, but it's also good self-care. Happy, healthy counselors = happy, healthy clients. It's contagious.

The other kind of self-disclosure (the good kind) is called a professional disclosure statement. It's a document, usually included with your intake forms, that shares a little bit about your counseling philosophy, your personal counseling boundaries, and the rules of your office. Not every counselor has one, but I'll venture to say most do, because it's a helpful way of setting the tone of the counseling relationship. Read on and decide for yourself whether you think it will be useful for your life.

Your professional disclosure statement should not be more than two pages (or one front-and-back) simply because your client won't read more than that. They may not even read your 2-page professional disclosure statement! You can try pushing this page limit, but I think you'll be disappointed. Hopefully they read every word. But if they don't and still choose to sign, at least later on you can truthfully say you gave them the opportunity to read your rules and boundaries.

So what might a professional disclosure statement look like? I've included a copy of the professional disclosure statement I used at the Family Counseling Center in *The Beginning Counselor's Survival Guide Workbook*, which you can purchase by going to www.stephanieadamslpc.com and clicking on the link to the Beginnings Store. A standard professional disclosure statement could include any of the following:

- Your credentials
- Your theoretical orientation
- Your hours of operation
- Contact information
- How you prefer to be addressed
- Risks and benefits of counseling
- Termination policy
- Cancellation policy
- Payment policy
- Explanation of confidentiality and limits of confidentiality
- Where to complain (if not already on your intake forms)

- Opportunity to designate and emergency contact person and/or define the terms under which they may be contacted

You could create a professional disclosure statement based on this list, but what I'd suggest is that you search other counselor's websites and read their professional disclosure statements. Don't copy word-for-word, of course, but pull out elements that you think are important to include. This way, you can create the exact right professional disclosure statement for the kind of counseling YOU want to do.

SOME ADVICE ON GIVING ADVICE

Read this book straight through and do everything it says.

Now, are you realistically going to do that? I would guess you had one of two responses: "Nobody tells me what to do" or "Yeah...sure. I'll get back to you on that." Fact is, you wouldn't just blindly follow my advice. (Nor should you.) You'll read over the book, take what you need, and shelve the rest. That's exactly what your clients will do with your advice. As odd as it may sound, that's a good thing.

Some people think that getting advice is what therapy is for. Really, it's not. We're not in the business of spoon-feeding people. We exist to give the client options they cannot see for themselves. Not dictate to them their life choices. If all you give out is advice, you will unintentionally create a relationship of dependence. (It is unintentional...right?) Your clients won't be able to think for themselves because they've always just had information delivered to them.

There is also the reality that no one can be perfect all of the time, and if you regularly give out advice, eventually you WILL come up short. Somebody will take your advice, and it will backfire. That's why you have to be careful. You don't deserve to lose your license over one bad piece of advice. So be careful. Give clients *options*, not advice, always making sure they know they have a choice. Your clients will appreciate you for it.

CHAPTER NINE
BOUNDARIES IN THE THERAPEUTIC RELATIONSHIP

THE DIFFERENCE BETWEEN BEING A FRIEND AND BEING A COUNSELOR

For new therapists, it can be difficult, even awkward, to define the relationship between themselves and their clients. Thousands of questions run through their minds. How nice is too nice? Am I doing enough for them? Is a hug inappropriate? Is withholding a hug inappropriate? Should they call me by my first name?

To some degree it's up to the individual therapist how they choose to answer these questions, depending on what they're comfortable with and who they are as a practitioner. There are certain ethical issues, however, that are inviolable. A lot of these will be discussed in the rest of this chapter, others will (hopefully) be obvious, and for the rest I will refer you to the dominating ethical code for your discipline and state. (For example, I chose the ACA Code of Ethics since I worked towards my counseling license, you might choose the ethical code of the ASCA if you are a school counselor.)

The therapeutic relationship is unlike any other out there. A close comparison might be the doctor/patient relationship, but while your doctor shares your medical history, you are not going into your most intimate thoughts and emotional traumas with him or her on a regular basis. Therapy usually happens once a week, like a friendly catch-up over coffee, but you can't make the mistake of treating your sessions like a coffee date. Our clients are not our friends. They can't be.

To take on the mentor role that we provide for our clients would be inappropriate in most friendships. Counseling is ultimately an unequal relationship. It is all about the client, and that's how it's supposed to be. But, that would not be satisfying for one of the people if this were a friendship. Additionally, the leeway allowed friends – calling whenever they need something, popping by unexpectedly, sending each other cards and letters, attending parties together – would be way over the line for a therapist and their client.

Logistically, making clients into friends would be way too much for most full-time therapists. Think about it. Can you really give 20-25 clients a week (the norm for many counselors) the full attention and time you give to your friends? It sounds exhausting to me. If you tried to do this each of your clients would feel deprived, because you wouldn't have enough to go around. This is not to mention the toll it would take on your non-client friendships as well. Your client also cannot be your friend because your client does not need to know that much about your life. It's not that you have anything to hide, but every piece of information you share with your client is another piece that could potentially reduce your effectiveness as

Carol's Comments: Clients want and need you to be out of their normal lives. Some drive longer distances to see therapists who they won't run into in the grocery store. The last thing they need to worry about is you.

a therapist. Think about it. If they find out something they like about you, such as a mutual interest in movies, perhaps, the session can potentially turn into a chat about the merits of Roman Polanski instead of an in-depth discussion of the client's issues. This is a problem because they are not paying you to hear about your taste in movies. Still, some therapists would put up with it. It's the client's time, and their choice, they would say. Maybe so, but are you doing them any good?

And of course, the more information they have about you, the more they feel they know you. In some instances, this can be a positive situation, creating camaraderie. ("Yes, I disagree with my husband on that issue too!") But it also has the possibility of creating distance between you and your client. For example, I went to Baptist schools, and that can create fear on the part of gay and lesbian clients that I will immediately dismiss them because of my religious beliefs. Unfortunately, that is a connotation of information I cannot change, because where I went to school is a part of my professional identity. But because people know this fact, sometimes I have to take up session time to explain that I am not here to judge or label them, I am here to listen and help them with what they *choose* to be helped with.

Any difference in beliefs or preferences can create distance between you and your client. That is the opposite of what we are trying to accomplish. Clients need to hear about your personal life only as it is directly related to developing rapport or encouraging their growth. Other than that, a therapist should be a blank slate.

Thinking like this can feel mean to some people. Holding a client at arm's length (seemingly) can resemble rejection. And unfortunately, many of your clients may take the implementation of boundaries as a personal rejection. But it still does more good than harm to maintain professional boundaries.

The people who come into your office often have no idea of what a healthy relationship is. Therefore, they are vulnerable. You may well be the only healthy person they know. You *must* clearly define your relationship and model healthy behavior for your client. It is what's good for them, and it's why they come to you. Clients are paying us for a window into a world in which they are well adjusted and content. We can create this new reality for them by using our words, but part of transmitting the message is by choosing healthy actions, too.

> Carol's Comments:
> Using examples from your own life can be helpful only if the focus is on the lesson that the client is currently struggling with and only if you don't talk more about you than about them.

Having appropriate boundaries in the therapeutic relationship tells a client that they can count on their therapist. They know what to expect. Most unhealthy people are erratic and arbitrary in their affections and expectations. You must be a steady, consistent force for those who have only been exposed to that kind of person. Many clients think a relationship must be "all or nothing," meaning either they put up with a person that they "love" despite their abuse or they reject everything about a person. You can show them that there is more than one definition of caring. Instead of being all-consuming, it can be balanced, professional and productive.

This is why we have to be careful about healthy client boundaries. Your client *deserves* a counselor, not a friend.

BOUNDARIES IN THE OFFICE

From the first phone call, it should be clear to a prospective client that this is a professional relationship developing between the two of you. However, the only way you can expect the client to know this is if you set the precedent by choosing to treat it professionally.

There are three major components to think about when conceptualizing appropriate boundaries in the office: stopping and starting on time, payment, and professional conduct.

Have you thought about what you will do if a client arrives late? What if it's a continual pattern? What if you're late? How long is your session meant to be, and how seriously will you enforce keeping it this long? Many counselors try to keep their sessions at 50 minutes. This is because they need those ten minutes to write notes, get a drink of water, and prepare for the next client. Will a counselor's day be ruined without those ten minutes? Of course not. But, after seeing six clients back-to-back with no breaks, a therapist can get pretty burnt out. It adds up.

If you don't schedule every hour on the hour, you may not choose to keep to the 50-minute mark. There's nothing wrong with that. You can structure your sessions however you choose. But when you do decide how long your sessions will be I recommend sticking to your decisions rather strictly. You want the client to see that you respect the time you have together, so that they will. It can be hard to tell a client "it's time to go," but it also keeps you accountable to make sure you use the session time wisely, since you know you will end in a timely manner.

Because I want my clients to respect the work we do in session, I don't keep them later if they don't arrive on time to our session. On the one hand, that might seem unfair because they're paying for 50 minutes. But the way things work is that they're paying for 3 pm to 3:50 pm. If they miss the first 20 minutes of the session, they still get until 3:50.

Of course there are real emergencies that come up that require flexibility on your part. But we are endeavoring to create a safe space in which the client can open up about what they're going through and receive the help they need. Not showing up on time is a sign of disrespect for that process.

Similarly, if YOU are the one who doesn't show up on time, you are showing that you do not respect the process either. I have had clients tell me they have worked with counselors before who cancel or reschedule weekly, sometimes not telling the client until the client was in the car driving to the appointment! That's not professional, and if you are unable to keep appointments on a regular basis, this isn't going to be the right career for you.

Another element that comes under the umbrella of office boundaries is money. Counseling is how you make a living. Therefore, you should expect to get paid for it. Unfortunately, there is a good deal of shame in the industry for asking to get paid for helping people. But just because we are helpers doesn't mean we don't have to pay rent. You don't expect to go see the doctor for free, do you? Most new counselors are in the process of paying off massive school debt. They also enjoy eating and putting gas in their cars. So if you are one of these people, let go of the guilt already. You're not going to be able to go forward with the rest of this section otherwise.

I can't tell you the right amount to charge per session. But I can tell you two major things to consider. First of all, does your site have a prescribed amount? There may be set rules about this kind of thing, and you can't get around it if you want to stay at this particular site. If you *do* have options about what to charge, think about what kind of income you need to make this business work for you. I can't guarantee you will get it, but you won't get it for sure if you don't plan for it.

You'll get a lot of conflicting information concerning what and how to charge people. Do sliding scale; don't do sliding scale. Some will say you must become an insurance provider, others will declare that cash-only is the new way to go! From what I can see, I don't think there is any pricing maxim that is universally true for every counselor, school counselor, marriage and family therapist, and addiction counselor out there. Just use common sense. If you are in a low-income area, it is very likely you will need to offer sliding scale and take Medicaid in order to keep going. Those in more upscale neighborhoods may be able to flourish with flat-rate cash-only fees.

> *Carol's Comments:* Research indicates people value what they pay for. Some tend to dismiss 'free' services as less valuable.

Towards the beginning of your counseling career, you may believe that you will only be able to bring in clients if you cater to whatever they want financially and personally. However, if we give them what they really want, we would be giving out free sessions and available 24 hours a day. In other words, you can't please everyone! Offer fair fees for your area, and have some standards by which you will choose to change them. People will respect that, or they'll go elsewhere.

After you decide how much to charge clients, another thing you should consider is when to collect payment. There are three basic options: at the beginning of session, at the end of session, or via billing at home. Some add a fourth option: not at all. By this I mean they give free consultations for the first-time client.

This is another area where you will hear opinions that are diametrically opposed to one another. I can see both sides of it. I would estimate about half of my first-time clients never come back again. I promise, that's not because I'm a terrible therapist! Especially for the beginning counselor, it's fairly normal to have a high number of dropouts. For established therapists, I gather clients are slightly less likely to defect so soon, simply because they invest more money in the process up front. That's the _problem_ I have with offering free consultations. But the _benefit_ is in giving clients a chance to see what they have to offer. As a new e-therapist, I chose to run a special offering a free email therapy session with no obligation to make any further appointments after that. Sometimes, when you're starting out, you might decide that giving away some of your time for free is the best way to build goodwill amongst potential new clients.

But on the downside, it also encourages clients to "sample" therapists with no commitment to the process. That's a waste of both of our time. If a client is willing to put down money, they are investing in making a change. So consider your options carefully. Which direction will raise your business to the next level?

The first time you meet with a sliding scale client, you may choose to take payment after session so that you can discuss qualifying factors for sliding scale beforehand. Otherwise, I don't really see the point in not collecting your fee at the beginning of session. It's not a major issue, by any means, but it does create some challenges. For one thing, the client is often emotional after a session. Sometimes they need to walk straight to their car and process. It could be embarrassing for them to have to stand in front of the receptionist and/or other clients to pay. For another, emotionally distracted clients might forget to pay, and others may choose deliberately not to pay. It's a lot harder to compel payment if they've already received the service.

I hear you saying, "But they have to pay me! I did my job!" Wouldn't that be nice? But, if you don't have an organized and effective system to collect payment, it will not happen on its own. It's just reality. Here's my line of thinking on delaying the billing process past the date of service. I don't particularly enjoy writing a check and putting it in the mail. The only reason I do it is I know that if I don't, bad things will happen. I will damage my credit rating if I don't pay my rent. Collectors could pursue me. So I pay my bills. But I still put them off as long as possible!

People often aren't being malicious when they "forget" to pay you. They're just being people. They got distracted, or another bill comes up, or they want to avoid seeing money come out of their account. Everyone has irresponsible moments.

For this reason, I hate the idea of sending collectors after those who won't pay me. Some therapists do it, and I don't fault them for it. But I hate it. And so that's why I make sure we collect on time and don't schedule new appointments until their payments are caught up.

What if a client does not show up for a scheduled session? Are you going to charge them late fees? For some situations and circumstances, we actually can't do this. Some government-funded reimbursement programs do not allow their providers to bill the client for no-shows. That's unfortunate, because fewer and fewer counselors are going to want to take on clients from these programs without that provision.

It's also problematic because, again, financial investment is a demonstration of respect for the process. With no financial penalty, why should they come into therapy when they don't feel like it? It doesn't affect them! I'm not advocating that we hogtie our clients into the therapy chair, or that we charge exorbitant late fees to ensure client participation. They still get to make their own choices. But if we believe in therapy, we have to do everything we can to encourage them to take it seriously.

Good reasons to waive late-cancel or no-show fees are reasons like sickness, flat tires, and children getting ill. Not-so-great reasons (which I have heard) include "But I forgot I had a meeting at work today" and "I got caught up doing laundry." To put it bluntly, is it fair that you lose out on income because of a client's household chores?

The worst feeling is when you choose to waive fees out of the goodness of your heart and end up getting burned because of it. I waived a fee once because the client told me they only had $30 in their checking account. I told them they could pay me next session. No-show, and I never got paid. Another client called the center on my day off, but I was the only counselor Debbie, our office manager, could reach at the time. It was a situation in which the client wanted advice about potential suicidality of a family member. I talked to her for free for an hour from my home phone, and then met with her later in the week. She told me she couldn't pay me that day, and then never showed up for our next scheduled appointment. That hurt, because I really cared about her situation, and I wasn't going to charge her for the phone call, just the session she came in for. But it was a lesson learned. Do not waive a fee unless you are ready to waive it *permanently*.

Answering the above questions results in the creation of healthy financial boundaries. Answering the questions following will create healthy office policies, which are another kind of boundary. However, there's not just one right answer to each question below. Some of it will depend on your therapeutic style. The most important thing is not that you answer in a certain way, but that you answer it in terms of your boundaries.

Will you allow guests of the client in the office for moral support?

Oftentimes clients bring a family member or a friend with them the first time they come to the office, because they are nervous. This generally doesn't carry on past the first session, so usually isn't a problem. Hear warning sirens, however, when an older teenager or young adult's parent is in the room and insists on telling the story for him or her. You can't conduct therapy without the client's participation!

What is allowed in your counseling office?

Do you have a problem with food or drink? If it is okay to have drinks, do they need to have coasters? What is your policy on whether client should text or take calls during your sessions?

Will you permit children in your counseling office?

I understand how difficult it is to get childcare. But if a client brings a child into my office, they might as well not come at all. Some might think that's putting it too strongly. But with the one exception being infants still nursing, any time I've had a child sit in on a parent's session it's been a disaster. The parent(s) spend half the time entertaining the child or keeping them

> *Carol's Comments:*
> *Children are tuned into their parents' feelings. Having a child in the office when a parent is talking about sensitive issues can distress the child.*

away from my desk instead of working through their issues. Many counselors' offices, also, are not childproof.

Parents can't finish their thoughts or be as honest as they need to be when their kids are around. (Little pitchers have big ears...and the memory of an elephant when you don't want them to!) If you read over this, but still come to the conclusion that you will not exclude children from parents' sessions, I'd recommend you think about ways to minimize the impact of what has just been discussed. Having coloring books or building blocks for them to play with can sometimes reduce the distraction.

BOUNDARIES OUTSIDE THE OFFICE

Did you know that your clients often live in the same city that you do? I know, it's weird to think about. Since we have to be so compartmentalized between our personal lives and our counseling lives, it's easy to forget that we can and will run into our clients outside of the office. It can be awkward, especially if you're wearing those holey jean shorts and a bandanna over your unwashed hair. But it can also be an ethical issue. We cannot wave, smile too brightly, or yell out our client's name in public. It may seem innocuous enough, but by doing so we are violating their privacy.

As I mentioned in the section on confidentiality, I put a sign up on my wall to let clients know if this situation occurs it is completely their choice whether to interact with me or not. The ethical thing to do is to leave it up to the client when you see them outside of your office. If they rush up to me to say hi, that is an indicator that they do not mind those around us knowing our relationship. (Still, I would probably double-check, "Can I have your permission to explain our relationship?" just in case.)

Keeping strong boundaries outside the office should also include limits and separation between personal information and professional information. By that, I mean on professional correspondence or interaction use only your office address, letterhead, email, phone number, and not your personal contact information. If you give that out, people <u>will</u> use it.

What are your work hours? Keep your interaction with clients within those hours. Yes, there are exceptions, but it's not healthy to always be on-call. I make a point of trying to not even reply to emails on weekends. It's very difficult for me, because if I see a job that needs doing I generally want to get it done right away! But if I start making a habit of answering emails on weekends and then don't reply on another weekend, clients will begin to become aggravated that I'm deviating from what I have done before.

What type of parameters will you set on doing your job outside of the office walls? (For you school counselors I will include the entire school building as your office walls.) Will you visit clients in their homes? Under what circumstances? Will you bill for travel hours if you do so? What about phone calls? Extended conversations can and do come up. Do you bill for them? Say, "let's save this for our appointment?" What about speaking with a client's doctor? Writing statements for court? Going to court? Parent consults? Is your head spinning yet?

If your site has guidelines on how to answer these questions, follow them first. If they don't, consult with your supervisor and decide what are the right options for you.

E-BOUNDARIES

Everyone has Facebook. (Even your parents, unfortunately.) If they don't have Facebook, they have a blog, or Twitter, or something else. We're all out there, just waiting to be found.

You've heard how potential employers will look at your Facebook page to see if there's anything particularly alarming about you before they offer you a job. That can be a scary thought. Now imagine emotionally troubled clients searching you out and viewing that picture of you bombed out of your mind on vacation, with the margarita umbrella tucked behind your ear. Yeah, your friends think it's hilarious, but do you think that will inspire many people to come to you for your support and wisdom?

Don't think they won't look you up. They will. Anything connected to your name is potentially available for clients to see. Some of that you may not be able to control. But what you can, you should alter immediately. If you can, deleting it is best. I'm a Facebook addict, so I dealt with it by creating a professional Facebook page and made my personal Facebook page private.

Even if you have a professional page, though, I would be careful with clients who want to "friend" you. It's fine for them to follow you on a professional level, "like" your page or read your Twitter updates. But if they friend you on Facebook, other people may ask them why they're friends with a therapist. And that can be a problem.

TERMINATION

Termination is the ultimate boundary. It tells clients, "We're done here. You don't need me anymore." In many ways this is a positive message, but it is also easy for clients to see it as a rejection, which is why it's so important to be clear and positive in communication.

In order for you to be positive in expressing the need to terminate, it's a good idea to know first for yourself why termination is advisable. It may be fairly obvious early on in the relationship: it might be that the client is someone with a situation you are not trained to deal with, or a client relationship that would create an ethical conflict for some reason.

But the main reason to terminate is that you're simply done working. You've helped the client with the issue they've come in to see you with, and they don't need your support any more to function successfully. It may seem counterintuitive to think about sending clients away, but the truth is the definition of being good at our job means at some point our clients will no longer need us. Besides that, our code of ethics mandate that we not persistently over-treat clients for our own gain. So it's not just a suggestion.

Here are a few ways you can tell your client is growing closer to readiness to terminate:

- You run out of things to talk about in session.
- Your client starts canceling or rescheduling often when they haven't done that much previously.
- Sessions frequently go off-topic, and client fills time with surface-level chatter.
- Neither of you are working towards a goal anymore.

If these things start happening, it is prudent to start testing the client to see if they are feeling the same way. Many times clients are hesitant to come out and say they don't think they need to come anymore, but are relieved when you are the one to bring it up. They are worried about hurting our feelings or being ungrateful, it's important that you assure them this is not the case. In fact, you will take it as a compliment!

> Carol's Comments:
> I tell my clients that I'm always working my way out of a job.

Your client has become attached to you over your time together, so it's better not to sever that attachment too quickly. If you can, I recommend spacing out sessions to two a month, then once a month, and then, "Call me when you need me." When you bring it up to them, state the situation in a positive way. "I've been noticing we're not working as much in session these days. I'm thinking that probably means that you're doing better right now. That might mean it's time to start giving you some more time to work through things alone." Another way to bring it up might be, "So, is there anything you are still looking for from our counseling relationship?"

While introducing this topic, I watch carefully to see how clients react, and encourage them with positive statements. "I believe you are ready. I know you can handle it. You have been doing so well on your own lately."

Sometimes even the most thoughtfully worded encouragement can still invite resistance. In these cases, it can be easy to question yourself, thinking that maybe your instincts were wrong. Be careful with this. While it is of course possible that you may have been jumping the gun by initiating termination, it is also just as likely that the client is reacting for other reasons. As I've mentioned before, you may very well be the first healthy relationship this client has encountered in their entire life. Let that sink in. Can you imagine now how terrifying it could be for a client to think they are losing something so significant? With compassion, remind them that they have something different now. They are different. They can create the healthy relationships they were missing for themselves.

Fear of change can also spark resistance. This is why I feel pretty strongly about being available to the client after termination. In effect, this usually only works out to being willing to be available, not actually interacting with them on a regular basis. Very rarely have I heard of clients that stay in constant contact with their therapists after termination. Most are done after they leave therapy, and find other things to occupy their time. But it's the knowing that makes the difference. Clients need to know that they can contact you, not necessarily that they will contact you. For that reason, if you change jobs, try to leave a forwarding address, email or phone number with your old place of business.

In some cases termination may require more boundary work. Lonely people may want your companionship, but if you kept your boundaries tight during therapy, they will know that you are not there to be their friend, but their therapist. If you think that you have a client that might be lost without your regular presence, it might be worthwhile to encourage them to find community resources in which they can build new relationships.

But there are two sides to every coin. It is also possible that the client may be the one that easily adjusts to termination, while the therapist struggles with it. I confess I still find myself sometimes thinking about teenagers that have been yanked out of my care, either by parents or circumstance, and wonder how they are. The sudden departures are like unfinished stories.

Counseling is a one-way relationship but emotions are a two-way street. It is natural to have feelings about clients you have come to care about, and don't let anyone criticize you for that. However, you must realize your limits, and respect theirs. If we're going to ask it of them, it's only fair that we follow the same rules.

CHAPTER TEN
POPULATION PRIMER

When you're starting your practicum or internship, you may think you want to work with a certain group of people. However, I guarantee you won't know for sure until you really work with them! I, for one, thought I would be doing marriage and family therapy when I started my degree. After my practicum, I realized what I really liked was premarital counseling and counseling with adolescents! (And who knows what other kinds of counseling I will grow to enjoy later on in my career?) Your ideas will evolve, as mine did. So that makes it a really good idea to expose yourself to as many different counseling circumstances as possible while in your practicum and internship. What better time to get the experience?

However, though I think you should see as many different scenarios as you can during this time, I don't want you to go in unprepared! That's why I included this chapter, which will help you prepare for many of the major groups of people (sometimes called "special populations") you might encounter. It's just a primer. You won't finish this chapter knowing everything, but my goal is for you to be armed with some helpful information when counseling any of the following populations. It's scary *enough* the first time you meet someone new and attempt to help them through whatever situation they are struggling with. There's no need to go into it unprepared.

In time, you will emerge with your own specialty, among the groups I'm about to mention, or others! Then YOU will become the expert, and I will be calling you for more information about what you know best! But for now, this is just enough to get you started.

DIFFERENT AGE GROUPS

Let's start with the most basic kind of categorization: age. Groups based on age can be divided many different ways. For today's primer, I'm going to separate them like this: play therapy clients, game therapy clients, teenagers, college students, middle-agers, and the elderly.

I call our youngest group the play therapy group because that's pretty much all you can do with them. Not that that's a drawback! Play therapy is a rich medium to explore emotions for both the child and the therapist. It teaches us to slow down and hones our observation and reflection skills. Not to mention that as a tool, it can be extremely effective. But working with this group can also be a major challenge. Very young children don't have the cognitive reasoning skills of an older child or adult. You can't sit down with a six-year-old and ask them to tell you what emotion is driving their sudden fits of rage. They're more likely to answer the question with, "I like purple" than they are to give a thoughtful response about their disappointment and lack of coping skills. It's not that they are unintelligent, it's just that their cognitive skills aren't developed to the level that they can comprehend this kind of question.

Learning play therapy is like learning a new language. Adults (ideally) work out their problems by talking them through, but kids work them out through play. You need different skills as a play therapist than you do as a talk therapist.

If you're planning on working with this age group, seek out classes in play therapy or read any of Dr. Garry Landreth's great books on the subject. You shouldn't have a problem working with this group if that's what you want, but you do need training before you get started. And you need practice before you start advertising yourself as an expert play therapist.

A difficulty in play therapy (or any therapy with minors) is working productively with the children's parents. Unfortunately, often the parent is a huge part of the problem. You teach the child one principle in play therapy: that their thoughts and feelings are valuable, that there are boundaries in life, or that it's okay to be sad sometimes...and then they go home and their parent demonstrates to them exactly the opposite!

So what do you do then? The best option, in my opinion, is to consult with the parent. Tell them gently what you're seeing, and listen to their perspective. In most cases, parents aren't really bad people. They are just worn-out, or they don't know what they're doing. If the former were the case, I would encourage you to listen to them and sympathize with their problem before doing anything else. It is enormously draining to be a parent. Ultimately, it's your responsibility as the child's therapist to tell them what you think the child needs. That's what they're paying you to do. But it's okay, and certainly therapeutically advantageous, to provide support to them. After you've shown them you truly care, you can collaborate with them to accomplish your goals for the child. If the parent is on your side, you're giving your child client the best chance of success.

The group I have dubbed the game therapy group consists of kids who are too old for play therapy ("that's for babies!") and too hyperactive to sit down calmly with you and discuss their problems. Any game that doesn't require too much cognitive processing is suitable for this purpose. There are specific therapeutic board games available for use with these ages, and sand tray therapy might also work especially well within this age range. The major advantage of games in general, though, is that they are a means of relaxing your client and helping them to see you as a friend. It's a way to communicate with them in a non-threatening manner. A lot of kids this age also enjoy drawing together while you talk to them, which can produce similarly positive results.

The one major thing this group has in common is rapid change. Eight to thirteen-year-olds care passionately about both forming their own identity and being a part of a group. They start to have feelings for members of the opposite sex at some point during this process, and develop a new appreciation of their peers' opinions. This means that you'll want to keep tabs on what they care about, because that's what gives you credibility. Make an effort to remember the songs and movies they like. But beyond that, you will want to encourage them to start making mature decisions and using logic to think through problems, because they're about to enter the stage when logic often goes completely out the window...

Ah, the teenage years. How glad I am that those are behind me. Working with teenagers in counseling, usually you either love it or hate it! Most of the time, I love it, although they can be an extremely difficult group. Some of what creates challenges with them is their general attitude about being there. Most of the time, showing up in your office is not their choice. You can't blame them. I wouldn't like my parents dragging me in to talk with a stranger either.

Also, by the time a teen has come into counseling with you, they've probably had a few experiences with authority figures that weren't so positive. Because of this, I believe it's important to be very clear with them about their privacy. Unfortunately, they haven't usually had a lot of it! At schools, people talk. When parents are worried, they have a tendency to share with friends and relatives, placing the teen under further scrutiny and subjecting them to questions like, "Why are you giving your mother so much trouble?"

Your client's parents have a right to read their underage teenager's session notes. But if you speak with the parents about the situation, often they will agree to back off to let you retain your client's trust. "Backing off," of course, is a relative term. I have had parents who, while never trying to read my notes, never failed to ply me for information in person! If you've discussed the situation with them previously, though, I think it's fair to remind them, "Hey, we agreed not to talk about this, remember?"

There are other common problems you'll run into with parents of teenagers:

- Sometimes parents don't tell the teen they're coming to counseling and then the teen is shell-shocked when they come in to meet you. Solution: Make this a part of the discussion when you first set up the appointment. Specifically, say, "Please make sure Sue is aware she is coming into counseling before you bring her in." You will be glad you did.

- They want results YESTERDAY. I can understand this. It's their baby, and they are afraid they will grow up and make bad decisions. But you will have to point out the triumphs you are making, because the parents will probably not see anything short of a miraculous overnight change as a success. Solution: Emphasize the <u>realistic</u> positive gains.

- They tend to grill the teen about your sessions with them. Try to head that off, if you can. Solution: Discuss early in parent consults.

- They think they're the client. They're <u>not</u>. The teenager is the client. Sometimes that might mean the parents get mad at you when you don't deliver the teen they thought they ordered. Solution: Manage expectations with the parents and focus on counseling with integrity to your teenaged client.

> *Carol's Comments:*
> Regardless of your particular theoretical approach, it is important to convey respect if you're working with teens. Respect is frequently demanded of teens by adults, but not always given. As a therapist, you'll get much farther if your teen client knows you know they're in a large part, driving their own lives.

Teens themselves are either up or down, like you or hate you. It's all or nothing. They may talk your ear off one session and then sit sullen and silent for the next one. Sometimes they might use you as justification for behaviors that you may not necessarily support. ("But Mom, Stephanie said I had to express my feelings!" after spray-painting the neighbor's car.) Try to take is a compliment even as you're frantically explaining to them that that wasn't exactly what you meant.

But all this is incidental. The most important thing I feel we can do as counselors for adolescents is listening. Really listening. I will get up on a soapbox here: I don't really feel that people tend to listen to teenagers much. Usually parents or teachers barely hear them out before switching over into lecture mode. (Not you school counselors or counselors who are parents of teens, of course. Other, more ignorant parents and teachers are the culprits here.) I'm not a parent, so I don't know how hard it is not to do so. However, what I do see is adolescents who have learned to expect a knee-jerk reaction, which means they will have more respect for you if you hear them out first.

Teenagers are *smart*. They know the hot-button words that usually get reactions out of adults: sex, drugs, suicide, gun, alcohol, party...and so forth. You have to bite your tongue. It's hardest when you get a situation in which a 15-year-old is asking you about safe sex. Every part of you may want to scream, "Are you kidding me? There's NO WAY you are emotionally mature enough to handle sex." You can't do it. It's what she expects

> *Carol's Comments:*
> I *am* a parent and I believe it's very important when working with teens and their parents— even when parents are making big mistakes— that counselors verbally acknowledge to the parent how hard this parenting gig is. Just stating the fact will help your adult clients know you're on their side, too.

you to do, and what will shut her down immediately. Instead, you have to respect her right to make her own decisions and give her everything she needs to know to come to the same conclusion on her own. When you're the parent, you can make the rules. (And you should. Teens need that too.) When you're the counselor, you listen and lead the teen to the right choice without telling them what to do.

College students, our next major group, may rarely encounter counselors outside of their own campus counseling centers. That's not a problem, because that's what it's there for. It just means that unless you're that kind of counselor already, you may not see them. But sometimes, when the campus counseling centers are full or they are seeking a particular kind of solution, they will call you instead.

This group in many ways can be a dream to work with. They're educated, often motivated, and enjoy thinking through their problems. But they also tend to deal with major insecurity about the future and overwhelming pressure in the present. (You remember that, don't you?) Because of this, I believe one of the biggest goals when working with someone in a higher educational program is to assess him or her for realistic self-appraisal. In the competitive world of higher education, people kill themselves over bad grades. They shoot their classmates. It's awful. Obviously, at some point the college student that committed suicide or homicide lost their perspective. That's why it's important to tell college students that this too shall pass, and they have many, many options still ahead of them.

Many people think that middle age automatically means a midlife crisis. While that's not necessarily true, there is a reason it's a cliché. Midlife is the time that many people begin to realize that inevitably, certain doors are closing to them. Families, age, and poor life choices can eliminate some options where previously there were no limits. This can be absolutely devastating if there the person has a much-desired goal that can no longer be achieved.

143

But middle-aged people still have many MORE choices still open to them! You even might know this yourself. A great deal of counselors today enter their careers later in life. They realized it was what they really wanted, and so they went for it. I think that's inspirational. Any of your middle-aged clients can similarly still make their dreams come true.

Carol has a way of putting it that is very appropriate. She tells people that five years from now they are still going to be five years older. So at that time, why not be doing what you want to be doing? It's never too late to make your life what you want it to be.

Encouraging a new direction is especially important for women who are experiencing empty nest syndrome. You pour your life into someone for 18 years, and then those ungrateful brats up and leave to live their own life! In reality, if a child leaves the nest it's a sign that the parents have done a good job rearing them, but I can understand why it doesn't always feel that way.

Many, many women reinvent themselves at this time, and I think that's fantastic. For women who are dealing with an empty nest, it's really important to reassure them that they still have value. They have another facet of their purpose, and it's time for that aspect to blossom!

Men also can get this empty feeling, but for them it's more often linked with retirement. Just like with empty nest, the activity that has taken up the majority of their week has suddenly been removed. It's not unusual to feel aimless, even if the retirement was much desired! It all comes down to finding a new sense of self.

It's important to do so before old age, as this can be an even more lonely and empty time for some people. Not only can seniors feel aimless due to their lack of regular work or child-rearing activities, but also physically they can't do what they could before. Their families may live farther away now. They start losing their friends. Depression is common.

Seniors who live longer and happier lives tend to lead active lives. They have regular social engagements, volunteer, exercise, play games, and visit family often. They learn something they've never learned before, or they travel. We have prescribed "activities" for each major age group in our society (marriage, children, work) but nothing after retirement. The successful counselor of seniors helps them find a meaningful purpose and build activities around that purpose.

DIFFERENT ETHNIC AND CULTURAL GROUPS

While some themes for the age groups above will be universal, most are standard for the American culture alone. We need a whole different set of rules for working successfully with another cultural group.

The most important thing to remember when treating a cultural group unfamiliar to you is to not take anything for granted. You are not in known territory, so let the client lead you. (That is actually a good rule for counseling in general...let the client lead!) If you have advance notice, read up on the ethnic history and values of your new client. Talk to someone you know of a similar cultural background. And ask the client how they would like to be treated.

Treating clients of different ethnic or cultural groups means that their goals may be vastly different than your own. It's great for a client to set his or her own goals. Our role is to support the client's wishes. But have you ever had someone set a goal that went really against your values? What about a goal that is theoretically opposed to your way of doing counseling? It's a lot harder to put into practice than it looks!

During my internship, I counseled a conservative Muslim woman who had been through severe abuse in her family of origin. As a result, she had anxiety, post-traumatic stress and trouble connecting with her husband and children today. In my system of treating anxiety, I believe the *first* thing you should do is to improve self-efficacy. I think it's essential to show your client that they can handle their own challenges.

Want to guess how well that worked for a client whose core values include women focusing only on their families and having the husband act as their major voice? Her husband was a very intelligent and kind man. I could tell immediately that he cared about her and wanted to support her in therapy. But he ended up talking for her in our therapy session. She was happy to let him do so, since she believed in keeping quiet in the presence of her husband. But it is very hard to treat a person you can't interact directly with.

I understood clearly what she cared about, and I respected her values. It wasn't a matter of client-to-counselor value mismatch, but instead a client-to-therapy mismatch. I didn't know how to do my kind of therapy under these particular circumstances. Whether through our incompatibilities or another reason, by the third session (and the first one we were able to conduct one-on-one) she told me she was feeling better and didn't need counseling anymore. I will never know if that was really true or if I had just failed to make a productive connection.

> Carol's Comments:
> Whether you're dealing with ethnic, religious or age-different clients, you as a therapist need to listen to their perspectives. You're also going to be listening for behaviors and beliefs that cause them difficulties. Both are important.

That was a hard one. I've learned in these kinds of scenarios that you have to respect the client's system. It's not our job to change their system unless the client brings this into the session as their main problem. If they're not vocalizing a desire to change it, we *have* to respect their background and work in a way that reinforces the way they live their lives. This rule applies to all races, cultures, and as we will come to see shortly, creeds.

SPIRITUAL CLIENTS

For the most part, counseling fits in very well with the evangelical and Baptist Christian worldviews. Counseling is gaining respect among other religions as well, especially Islam and Judaism. Nearly all religions have some organized system of support for their members, so no matter what your spiritual background; you could conceivably be able to perform counseling under that umbrella. These days, counselors are more and more often incorporating other modes of spirituality into their practice, even those that might not be otherwise formalized into a religion. Examples might be counselors who use Reiki or forms of hypnotherapy.

Because our country has a separation of church and state, if you are licensed by the state, you have to follow specific rules for performing spiritual counseling. One choice for Christian counselors is to avoid state licensure altogether, and choose one of many helpful Christian or Bible-based counseling resources. Most of the time, one of these options fulfills what a person wants to do very well. But if any religious person chooses state licensure, they MUST follow state guidelines in regards to religion and counseling.

The most important thing to remember is that you can't push your religion on your client. They are vulnerable, and you're in a position of authority over them. It's not a fair situation. There are two exceptions to this rule. If a person brings up their religion first, AND you happen to share it or support it, you can go forward using principles of faith to guide you. (This within reason – counseling is not church.)

The other exception is if you declare up-front that you will perform counseling in a faith-based manner. If they sign an informed-consent document, you're not taking advantage of them. It can be a perfectly acceptable niche market practice. There are many clients specifically seeking "Christian counseling."

Clients in general who have strong spiritual beliefs often bring up the "big questions" in counseling. You don't have to know all the answers to these questions, but it's helpful to prepare to for this eventuality. Like a person's cultural history, this is their lens and their background. It's naturally going to be a large part of who they are. A person's spirituality is not for you to change as a counselor. Instead, you must work within it. (Again, primarily faith-based counseling practices can advocate their beliefs more strongly due to the informed consent.)

> **Carol's Comments:**
> When you've found a belief system that really helps you, it can be hard not to press this on others. You have to remember, however, that the biggest gift is your assistance. Every client won't have the same values and you need to accept this. When clients' belief systems significantly violate your own, though, you might want to consider referring to another counselor.

It might surprise you that you can still work very well with someone who believes something different than you do. Though I am a Christian, I connected with the Muslim couple I mentioned previously on the fact that faith governs much of our lives. I was able to have a lively discussion with a client who believed in Buddhist principles by realizing that looking at the big picture and the search for meaning in our lives were two things we had in common.

In reality, sometimes having a client with a different belief system can be easier than counseling one with the same beliefs as you have! I had a frustrating therapeutic relationship with a fellow Christian who believed God wanted her to stay with a husband who was physically and emotionally abusive. Now, I don't presume to know everything that God thinks, but my beliefs told me that God wouldn't want her to be hurt! I encouraged her that if she truly felt she should stay married, to work towards that while keeping herself physically safe from her partner. She wasn't interested. In her mind, she knew what God had told her. Probably there are a lot of people of my faith that would back her up in that, but I didn't. It just goes to show you that no matter what you share, no one is going to agree with you on every point. That's why it's important to realize that you're not here to get them to concur a point, but to reach a healthier place.

GLBTQI CLIENTS

I am going to discuss some of the unique needs of Gay, Lesbian, Bisexual, Transgendered, Queer and Intersex clients in this section. But before I do that, I also want you to see the ways in which they are not unique as well. What do I mean by that? I think so many people who aren't acquainted with the GLBTQI population get the perception that this community has one particular set of challenges and one particular mindset. While it's true that they have some unique challenges that are common and limited to their group, at the same time, they're still just regular people! Gay and lesbian couples have the same communication issues that straight couples do. They have in-law problems. They argue about parenting. So when looking at their distinctive needs, don't forget the ones they have in common with everyone else!

The major "distinctive" issues I suggest you tune in to when working with GLBTQI individuals or couples are legal concerns, social perception and isolation. When I say "legal issues" I am primarily referring to marriage and adoption. Some states allow gay marriage, and some couples get married in Canada before moving back to the U.S. Does your state of practice honor these marriages and subsequent privileges? What about divorce? (Yes, gay marriages do end in divorce at similar rates to straight marriages.)

If the couple has children, how are the rights to the children governed? Having children is a fundamental demographic characteristic for any client, but for GLBTQI individuals it can take on a lot more significance. Parents who have formerly had children in straight relationships can lose custody after coming out. Adoption can be put off in cases where two women or two men are raising a child or children, until it's too late. I once saw a lesbian client that stayed home with twins that her partner gave birth to. When the relationship went south, she was in danger of losing custody of the children (who after all, knew her as the primary caregiver) because she had not yet legally adopted them. That is traumatic for both the excluded partner and the children.

For gay, lesbian and bisexual clients, public perception and acceptance is a constant concern. You will probably want to question clients about their family's reaction to their coming-out, or if the family even knows about it. This will tell you a lot about what kind of support system they have in place, if any. Their sexual orientation may impact their ability to remain employed, although that's becoming less and less of an issue without recourse as legal measures are put into place to protect against discrimination.

It's often harder for a GLBTQI person to start relationships because they don't know how a person might react to advances. Rather than graciously saying, "Sorry, I'm straight," some people meet same-sex romantic overtures with ridicule or violence. This could impact how a person perceives future relationships.

Transgendered clients have just as difficult a path to walk. Individuals identifying as transgendered often describe themselves as having been born in the wrong body. I suggest you try to imagine what it would feel like for you to be in the same situation, in order to help you relate to them. For me, I like being a woman! I cannot imagine if I were to have the physical body of a man. It would be hard to feel like such a fundamental thing about me was off-balance. And that's the feeling they struggle with every day.

Transgendered is a poorly defined term. Sometimes it can refer to someone who is currently feeling gender dysphoria, but it can also used interchangeably to indicate someone who's already undergone gender-reassignment surgery. In order to clarify what your client means by this term, I might ask them, "So what does transgendered mean for your life personally?" It's more respectful, in my opinion, to define the term with them than to make assumptions.

Your role as a counselor will be different whether the person is considering changing their gender, has already done so, or is just at the stage of struggling with it. Transgendered people do not necessarily follow a linear path. Some may deal with the internal conflict by cross-dressing but never seek to change their body. Ask the client what they want, and don't assume they're seeking to either get gender-reassignment surgery...or that they aren't, either! Everyone is on a different journey.

A transsexual client (gender-reassigned) once told me that he was taught if he took the surgery option, he would have to say goodbye to everyone he knew and basically start over. After experiencing the change, he said that was a correct statement. He became isolated from his family, who didn't know how to relate to him when their sister was suddenly a brother. It's often difficult to re-form a relationship with children after surgery. His son still chooses to call him "Mom," and he's fine with that. Thankfully, he's been able to still have a relationship with him after the change, but it was a rocky road.

Choosing which gender-specific pronoun to use when speaking about the client is nerve-wracking for some therapists. Carol wisely told me when I confessed to worrying about it to just ask the client what they preferred to be called, or to go with what other people used for them. If a pre-op female who felt male was still referred to as "she" by her mother in family therapy, it would be appropriate to still use "she" when discussing the case in supervision. The transsexual client I mentioned above was a male physically and emotionally, so there wasn't a question whether or not to use "he" or "she" in his case.

Writing this section so soon after the spirituality section makes me very aware of the controversy over counselors of faith treating GLBTQI clients. The law in regards to counseling in opposition to your belief system is ill-defined. Some schools have expelled counselors for refusing to treat GLBTQI people on basis of their religion. I have heard from some that have stated it's something that counselors just need to "get over." I don't know if I feel it's fair to compel a counselor to do something against their belief system, just as I wouldn't force a client to do something against theirs. However, I offer another perspective to consider. I'm a Bible-believing Christian, but I don't choose to eliminate any potential client. My religion is "out there" because I went to Baptist schools. My clients can see this on my degree certificate. But *I* believe my role is to counsel, not to convert. Counselors help make the client's goals a reality, whatever those goals are, however much they agree or disagree with the counselor's beliefs.

I did not want to reinforce the stereotype that Christians hate people that are different from them. For me, the right choice was NOT to perpetuate that idea any more. *Another counselor's choice may be different.* Before you begin seeing clients, it's important to know for yourself how you are going to deal with potential worldview conflicts and treat everyone involved in a respectful, ethical and lawful manner.

SUICIDAL CLIENTS

If you're like me, you used to dread getting a suicidal client. Maybe you still do. But it's part of the job, and we have to be prepared for it. Especially with clients that are considering taking their lives, we have to be on top of our game.

First, memorize the suicidal checklist. Don't know what this is? Shame on your school, then! The suicidal checklist is a body of questions that helps counselors assess the likelihood that a client will commit suicide. (Look it up by typing "Suicidal Checklist" or "Suicidal Assessment" in a search engine.) It helps us to know when we need to call the police and when a client might just be "talking it out."

The right way to ask the checklist questions is to work them in to the conversation. Your client may clam up if they perceive that you are running through a list with them. The questions on the checklist focus on assessing means and motive. How is the person planning to kill themselves? If they are mentioning a specific method, do they have access to that method? For example, if a person plans on ending their life by gunshot, but they don't have a gun, they are at relatively low risk for suicide. Conversely, a person who lives on the 35th floor and plans to end their life by jumping off a building is at *significant* risk of hurting themselves.

Another question you will want to ask is if the person has thought about suicide before. If their answer to that question is yes, use that response as a springboard to find out what stopped them when they were considering suicide previously. When they tell you what kept them from it in the past, lean on that. Don't be afraid to make judicious use of "guilt" here. Your number one job is to keep them alive. If they don't want to kill themselves because they have children, let them know that statistically kids of parents who commit suicide are more likely to commit suicide themselves. Of course, don't say, "If you kill yourself it will be your fault if your kids do too!" Instead, show them that because of the fact that children often model their behavior after their parents, if the parent chooses to carry on despite a painful situation, they can teach their children that they can keep going in difficult times, too. Encourage them to live as a way to inspire their children and protect them from later self-harm.

Religion comes into play here. If they have the perception that suicides go to hell, now might not be the time to enlighten them if you disagree. I'm not by any means suggesting that you lie... but be smart. What's going to help them see suicide as a poor option? Go with that right now. You can discuss that with them later if you feel it's necessary, when they're in a more stable place. Your job now is to find the wall that's preventing them from choosing suicide and build it even higher.

Another clue often mentioned as an indicator for suicide is when a person suddenly begins giving away significant possessions, or displays sudden cheerfulness after weeks of despair in session. Your instinct might lead you to think the latter factor means the person is feeling better, but beware. Sometimes the mental torment of considering suicide produces the anguish you see, and the sudden calm after all that means that the person has made the decision to kill themselves, and is now experiencing peace. In cases like this, move immediately back into assessment mode. Reflect the sudden change in their mood, and if at all possible, tell them what you think it means. They may or may not tell you if you have guessed correctly. But all you can do is give them an opportunity to talk about it, and hope they allow you in.

Something I often say to suicidal clients is that it is their right to end their life if they so choose to. Why? Because I don't want them to kill themselves just to prove they can! I quickly add to this statement that it is NOT the choice I would choose for them, and I think there are better options out there. But I want to give them insight into their autonomy, because feeling in charge of one's own destiny is essential for suicidal individuals. If you can help them see that they have the choice to kill themselves, you can also help them see that they have other, more positive choices.

Carol taught me a few phrases that often help in circumstances like these. One is sharing with them that, "Suicide is the last choice you will ever make."

> *Carol's Comments:*
> *Because counselors are sometimes sued by grieving, angry family members, the perceived risk to them goes beyond their concern for the suicidal clients. It's our job, however, to focus on the individual in the counseling room. I've always found it important to remember that suicidal thoughts are usually a response to a life situation that is perceived as overwhelming. Most clients don't want to die; they want the pain, distress, or difficulty to go away.*

Another is that, "If things get better tomorrow, it's too late. You're already gone." In my experience, these phrases really seem to help suicidal people consider their situation in a different light. Suicide comes from emotional desperation. Often when a person is considering suicide, the thinking part of their brain is temporarily turned off in the face of extreme emotional distress. Asking questions that require logic to answer can sometimes re-activate that thinking so they can make more balanced decisions.

In preparing for work with suicidal clients, sadly you also need to be aware that clients on occasion might be crying wolf. I don't say that to seem callous. But unfortunately, some people say, "I want to kill myself" when really they mean, "I'm sad and I don't know how to talk about it" or "I'm tired of the way things are," or even "I want attention." You might be alerted to the possibility that this is the case if previous suicide attempts or threats have been of a less lethal nature. Swallowing pills is a suicidal gesture, but it's considered a lot less lethal than an attempted suicide by hanging. One method leaves a window in which a rescue could be made, but the latter method rarely leaves a survivor.

I've been noticing that kids are picking up on saying, "I want to kill myself" of late as well. I had a client that was taken to the hospital by her mother before she came to see me, because she said she wanted to kill herself. As a result, by the time she came to see me, she was terrified to talk about her feelings. After all, the last time she did that she ended up in the hospital, poked, prodded and questioned. Did I mention this client was six years old? I ask you this: how exactly is a six-year-old going to follow through with that threat? In my experience, preteens and kids don't generally know what suicide means. By that I mean they may realize it ends in death, but they don't have a concept of a person actually killing themselves or a real desire to do it to themselves. What they do know is that it gets a reaction. Kids are smart that way.

Use good judgment in dealing with these cases. You do have to be really careful about this. If the child has been through really severe abuse or something else where they saw no escape, they might truly be serious about committing suicide. But outside of that, I see it as highly unlikely that they are truly contemplating killing themselves.

With all that said, it's still better to err on the side of being overzealous than not. You can never know for sure what a client is thinking. Always check with a colleague before deciding not to follow up with a police call about a suicidal client. It's not worth the risk not to do so. Write about the consultation with a colleague in your notes, especially what specific aspects of the situation that led the two of you to conclude not to notify the authorities. And follow the suicidality checklist, as the questions above are recognized as quality indicators of potential suicidality.

Remember you're not God, and you're not Superman. If a client is determined to kill themselves, sadly, no one can really prevent them from doing so. You can't lock them up forever, and clients who really are ready to leave life can easily lie to make sure their plans are uninterrupted. It's a very sad situation when this is the case. You should throw everything you have into trying to prevent suicide, but ultimately, you must realize that it is their choice. Seek counseling for yourself if you experience the death of a client from suicide. It's normal to have major feelings attached to such a huge loss. It's an absolute tragedy whenever someone gives up on his or her future. Anyone close to them will be affected by it. Including – and perhaps especially – you.

CLIENTS THAT NEED MORE HELP THAN YOU CAN GIVE

Even though I have no doubt you are or will be a very good counselor, there will be some clients that you cannot treat. I bring this to your attention now, at the beginning of your career, so that you will feel more empowered to help these kinds of clients in ways you can, and find them outside help for the ways you cannot. It will be a lot less stressful on you if you if you know this up front, and you will ultimately be a more effective counselor for it.

Let me give you some examples of clients that you cannot help completely on your own. First, clients with eating disorders. Talk therapy and family therapy are great for clients with eating disorders. But there is a huge medical component to eating disorders you will simply not be trained to handle. You can't monitor potential physical issues, like heart problems, proper nutrition, and esophageal damage from purging. You will need to work as part of a team with medically trained professionals to help a client battling an eating disorder.

Similarly, you can definitely help a client who has addiction problems as a general-practice counselor, but you don't have what they need to help them through physical withdrawal and detox. Depending on your facility, you may also not be able to support group therapy, which is a commonly-used and effective addiction treatment protocol. This is also a group of people you will want treat in the context of an integrated system of care.

Another example would be a case in which the problem is not emotional, but related to brain function. Try as you might, you cannot cure schizophrenia with talk therapy. After medical treatment, you might be able to help them deal with their feelings about having the disorder, as well as how it impacts their family relationships. But before medication, it's unlikely they will consistently make appointment times or hold on to what you have talked about for a long period of time.

When you come across cases like these, don't feel badly that you are not able to do more for them. You know people who do, and you will help your clients find them. That's all you can do. You don't blame yourself that you can't perform an appendectomy, so don't beat yourself up over an inability to perform these other tasks you are not trained to do.

DIFFICULT CLIENTS

What makes a difficult client? Oh, just brace yourself. These examples may frighten you (as well they should) but don't despair. Every example of a Scary Mary or a Horrifying Harry I share with you is an opportunity for you to begin asking yourself, "What would I do if this happened to me?" Preparation is power. I've given you some ideas for how I've dealt with it in the past to get you started.

Clients Who Don't Respect Your Expertise:

Several of the following examples of difficult clients will apply to counselors of every level of experience. But this particular one is all our own. One of the hazards of being an intern is that everyone knows you're an intern. Everyone's nervous when they start out, but some clients will smell it on you. The nice clients will choose to stick with you while you figure out your style. The ones who don't really want to be there may decide they'd rather use it against you.

> *Carol's Comments:*
> It can frequently help to refocus a session and pull a client away from lecturing you if you simply ask in the middle of a challenging interaction, 'Why are you here?' This needs to be done without anger and with respect, but the message is clear—the clients wouldn't be there asking for your help if they had all the answers. Be prepared, though, for some clients to say that they're in your office only because some significant other person" made" them come. This is a great opening for you to talk about that relationship and to reflect the clients' frustration with feeling forced into therapy.

This problem is compounded when you're on the younger end, like I was when I started. My first counseling session, I was 23 years old. I got a lot of sideways looks that said (roughly) "excuse me? Just what do you think *you* know, missy?"

Maybe you've been asking yourself the same question. But you'll have to stop, because what helps clients that think you're full of it is for you to know that you are not! When you're a newbie, you don't always have faith in yourself. But you've got to overcome it, or else your fear will stop your new career in its' tracks.

Remember this: you have a degree. You are progressing towards a professional license. In other words, you are kind of a big deal. So remind yourself of that once in a while! Don't take any flak. At the very least you have the benefit of having an objective, third party perspective on their problem. Nobody can see his or her own life objectively. They *need* this from you.

Also, don't take it too seriously when you do get disrespected. I was able to get past it when I decided to start taking it as a challenge. When I felt disdain for me or for something I said creep in, something would go off inside of me and I would say to myself, "Oh really? Well let me show you just what I can do!" It got to be an expectation I looked forward to inverting, as a personal challenge.

If you project confidence, your clients will interpret that confidence as expertise. You can do it!

Clients Who Monopolize and Interrupt:

Sometimes I find myself in a session where I'm asking myself if I even need to be there. My client is barely pausing to take a breath, and even if I interrupt back, he or she stares at me for a second without comprehension before resuming their breakneck pace.

Oh, this is a hard group. There's two warring factions inside you as the therapist when this happens: the desire to let your client talk it out, and the urgent need to contribute something, anything, just so long as you're not sitting there with your mouth hanging open!

In my experience, there are usually only a few reasons that this happens. The person might be nervous to be in therapy and afraid you will judge them. Not allowing you to talk becomes a defense mechanism. These cases usually solve themselves, as your client gets more comfortable with you.

Another reason is if the monopolizer is a member of a couple or a family therapy session. You'll know if you have one of these because their speeches will solely consist of examples of how they've been wronged by the other party in counseling with them, and of course what you as the counselor should tell other party to do better. Some counselors prefer to let these kind of people expel their energy and then balance it out later on, but the danger there is that you alienate the other party by seeming to take the monopolizer's side. You can also choose to intervene and say, "Thanks for sharing, let's hear how _____ responds to what you just said." Fair warning: You might have to do this the entire time they are in counseling with you.

It's also a possible strategy in either of the above situations to point out what they're doing and ask them what they think it means. Having them define the monopoly in their own terms makes sure you're not labeling them, and provides the client an opportunity for insight.

Another approach might be to ask them what they're here for. When they respond "to help our marriage" or "to stop feeling _____," you then have an opening to say. "Oh, if that's what you're wanting, I'm going to talk more about _____ in order to make that happen." Once you've prepped them, you have obtained permission to rely on that reason the next time you have to interrupt. "I appreciate what you're saying, but I promised you we were going to touch on _____ so let's do that now."

Clients Who Are Rude:

Yes, this happens. Unfortunately. Some clients don't want to be there, so they're going to make sure you don't want to be there either. Some are just really angry, with everyone they come into contact with. Some are habitually rude people, and you're just another person who gets to share in the unpleasantness they're spreading.

Take heart. Though it might be difficult if your place of employment doesn't back you up on this, I don't believe you have any obligation to work with rude people. Part of your job as a counselor is to help them function in the real world. And if they treat people this way in the real world, there will be consequences. So there should be with you.

When possible, it's good to confront them on that in a considerate manner. "You know, I really want to help you, but the way you're talking to me is making it harder." If the behavior persists after that, or the person starts cussing you out, you have my permission to hang up on them or show them to the door.

Sound harsh? Hey, you could be screaming back at them. (By the way, don't do that.) Let's talk about positive and negative reinforcement. If you keep pleading with a person who's being unnecessarily rude and isn't showing you any signs of working with you, they're going to make the connection that it's *okay* to keep doing this. It's not! The only way they get this message is to remove the reward: your attention. If they find they don't get to talk to you when they scream at you, they'll either stop screaming or go away. Either is better than being screamed at.

> *Carol's Comments:*
> Never let yourself slide into feeling like a victim of your clients. You have choices; you don't have to continue seeing clients who are an infliction and if you feel this way about all your clients, you deserve a break and your own counselor. Everyone feels this way sometimes, but you don't have to continue a career that really doesn't work for you.

You have a responsibility to your other clients to be a healthy counselor. Good self-care involves saying no to people who are verbally abusing you. Enough said.

Clients Who Want to Please the Counselor:

I know it seems mean that I'm going to tell you how to eliminate the one situation that actually is a little more fun for us as counselors: the ones who want to make us happy. These are the ideal clients in some ways. They come to session on time, they do all the homework you assign, and they flatter you constantly about how much you are helping them. It can feel really good to you!

But it isn't good for the client.

We do want our clients to do their homework, and to come to session on time, and maybe just a little we want them to tell us how great we are as a therapist. But if they're doing it for the wrong reasons, they're not actually benefitting from your therapy. When the relationship is over, they won't do things that are good for them anymore. That's because they did them for *you*, not because they saw any actual value in them themselves.

An example of a "wrong reason" why a client might try to please their counselors is that some individuals are compulsive people pleasers. They put everyone else first and subjugate their needs. You want to work against that, not accidentally encourage it.

Another scenario might involve a client that is intentionally or unintentionally avoiding the real issues. Who are we generally harder on, people we like, or people we don't? When we're caught up in all the warm fuzziness, we can forget to look for what they're not telling us.

You have to be stronger than all this. Set boundaries. Address it directly. Always affirm that you do care for them – as you do all your clients – but therapy is about THEM, not you.

Clients Engaged in Self-Pity:

Poor me! This is the perception that most civilians hold about counseling. I believe many people think that we get these kinds of clients all the time. Not true. In my experience the clients who throw pity parties are thankfully few and far between. Everyone has their moments, but I would say the majority of my clients spend most of their time working instead of feeling sorry for themselves.

That's the main issue when you're dealing with this kind of client. Yes, it's hard to have patience with somebody who is constantly saying "poor me," but more than that it means that they've conditioned themselves to be helpless. That's not only annoying to other people, it's really bad for *them*. If everyone is out to get them and their life is completely out of their control, then (in their minds) they have no ability to change their future.

That's what counseling is all about. Change. You might have to remind them of this – gently, of course. It's good to affirm that you believe in them, but not always effective with the real hard-core cases.

My advice with the pity-partiers? Drop your other work with them and focus on strengthening their internal locus of control and self-image first. You won't get anywhere until they master that.

Clients Whose Problems Work For Them:

Unfortunately, these are not quite as rare as the self-pitiers. In counseling, you'll see a lot of people whose problems "work for them." What do I mean by that? I mean that they are receiving some kind of benefit for the problem they're supposedly seeking to change. They may not realize it, or they may be completely conscious of what they're doing.

A classic example might be when a woman who is being abused by her husband or boyfriend continually returns to him despite his abusive behavior. She comes in to see you saying she wants to leave him, but makes no move to do so despite weeks of hearing your encouraging suggestions. The hidden benefit (or, what "works" for her) here could be one of several things: she feels loved when the man enters the "honeymoon" phase of the abuse cycle and showers her with affection to make up for his earlier abuse. She feels sorry for him and gets value out of the idea of rescuing him. She enjoys being the victim. (Note I am not making a blanket statement about all those who are subject to abuse, just a possible example.)

There are only a few things you can do here. First, try to bring your client into an awareness of what you think she's doing. I find it helpful and nonthreatening to put it in terms of costs and benefits. "You want to leave him because he's abusive *(cost)* but you feel so loved when he wants you back *(benefit)*." Share how it is logical and natural to want benefits, but she has to decide whether the costs are worth the benefits.

You can emphasize how long-term, the costs will stack up, and the potential benefits can be had from following another path. You can work with her transplant the benefits she's receiving from her abuser to benefits from another source: a women's group, a community program, or a family member.

Your challenge as a counselor is to see how you can make this kind of client's problem *stop* working for them, so they can achieve the goals they brought in to counseling. Good luck!

CORE COMPETENCE THREE: COUNSELOR SELF-CARE

CHAPTER ELEVEN
COUNSELOR, HEAL THYSELF!

WHY THE COUNSELING PROFESSION?

Why is a good question for clients and counselors alike. Why that feeling? Why that choice? Answering "why" helps a person own their decision. Which is why (there's that word again) I ask that same question of myself from time to time.

I think it can be assumed that I enjoy my job. I wouldn't write a book about it if I didn't! But even with that being the case, I still find it important to review my reasons from time to time. What about you? After all, you didn't just take a left turn and end up with a degree in mental health. Something drove you to this point. Something made you choose this job over a hundred others. Something made you into a counselor.

A lot of people will be answering to themselves right now, "Why, that's easy! I got into it to help people." Sorry, that's not going to be enough of an answer today. Don't get me wrong: that is in no way a bad reason to get into something. But there are tons of other ways you could have chosen to help people. Start a nonprofit. Enter the medical field, the police force or the military. Become a foster parent. Why was this way the right way for you? Why this field?

Carol's Comments:
This is a very personal issue. We all have our reasons for choosing this job. I once told my daughter, who was in an 'aha' moment after we talked, that the look on her face at her realization was why I went into therapy.

I'm going to go out on a limb here and say that the only right reason to do this is because you "have" to. By that, I mean you've surveyed or experienced other career paths and you've found that nothing comes close to the feeling of helpfulness and satisfaction you get from studying and practicing counseling. *Why* should that be a focus for consideration? The reason is that you're going to be doing it for the rest of your life.

My "have to" moment came freshman year of college. I had a vague idea of wanting to help people (See, I understand!) but was planning on family law, not psychology. At the time, I was a declared political science major. As it turns out, I could not have been more wrong about what I was meant to do. I started getting a clue that I might ought to consider a new direction when different girls in my dorm started coming to me, unbidden, to talk about their problems.

Now, I know you might be thinking that this is pretty normal for girls that age. True, but I was not what one could call a social butterfly. There was no reason why some of these girls would seek me out. I certainly had friends, but I also kept to myself and spent a lot of time at the library. Still, girls from different floors ended up in my room, cross-legged on the floor, pouring out their souls to me. I heard about childhood sexual abuse, school problems, and boyfriend issues among many other things.

It just happened, and I started figuring out I liked being a person of confidence. I wanted to help, even if it was just by listening. Some of those girls never spoke in depth to me again, but I still felt pleased and satisfied that I was able to be there for them when they needed help. By sophomore year, I was a family psychology major. And the rest is history.

When was your "a-ha" moment? When did you know for sure that you wanted to spend your life counseling? When did you decide that years of study and a lengthy internship were worth doing this for a living?

Many people make the choice to be a counselor because they themselves, or someone in their family, has struggled with mental illness. Who knows how many counselors owe their career to a bipolar parent? Sometimes, there is some element of shame associated with this particular reason for becoming a counselor, more so if the one affected by mental illness is the person who became a counselor.

Stop. There should be no shame associated with dealing with emotional problems as a helping professional. We are people too, and as prone to such problems as anybody else. The only thing you must be responsible for in this position is to make sure that your own struggles are not interfering with the work you do as a counselor. Other than that, having a background of mental health problems can actually be a bonus as a professional counselor today.

Why? Having had problems in your past, you have more credibility in your work today. You've been through this before. You're not just giving advice from a position of cold clinician; you are coming from a role as a fellow survivor of a major emotional problem. The word survivor is an important one. Do not underestimate how powerful it can be to your clients to hear that not only have you been through something similar to what they've been through, you've gotten through it and are helping other people with problems.

> *Carol's Comments:*
> *Your professors spoke about the importance of clients feeling understood— recognized. You're in a much better position to do this when you've accepted and understood your own process.*

I had a major depressive episode in college, strong enough that I sought counseling at school. I can tell you, I never felt lower or less worthy of the job I was (by that time) training for. But my counselor told me that what I was going through did not mean that I could not help other people. She told me exactly what I'm stating here, that it will actually only make me more understanding of others with the same problems. I had the chance to later encourage one of my clients the same way. She was also a college student who was considering counseling as a possible career, but struggled with depression. I wrote the counselor who had helped me in college on that same day I spoke to the student, telling my counselor that her advice and encouragement had now come full circle.

If you've had problems, or are currently having problems, don't think that precludes you from becoming an amazing counselor. Just make sure you deal with what you need to deal with before interacting with clients. If it's a recurring issue, consider getting counseling for yourself. There's no shame in it. This is what we do.

COUNTERTRANSFERENCE

Having a firm conception on why you do what you do is instrumental in preventing burnout, which will be discussed further in chapter thirteen. It's also very important in recognizing and defeating countertransference. This refers to situations in which a client's experiences, characteristics, or feelings trigger a reaction in the therapist related to something in the therapist's own life. This can be a problem whether that reaction is positive or negative. If negative, it can cause the therapist to be irritated with or have outright dislike for the client, halting effective therapy. If it's positive, on the other hand, it can cause the therapist to lose neutrality, encouraging them to react to the client based on an ideal rather than the real person.

My thesis throughout this book has been that we do therapy for ourselves; to satisfy a need we have and give us satisfaction from our work. But with countertransference I must make one distinction. The *work* of being a therapist is for us. The *therapy* we do is for the client. We cannot allow our own experiences to mute our effectiveness with a client, or we damage our integrity.

Countertransference has power when you are not aware of it. However, like vampires, (the Tom Cruise kind, not Robert Pattinson kind) it turns to dust when exposed to the light. The first thing to do in combat with countertransference is to be *aware* of your own reactions to clients. Do you like them? Do you dislike them? Do you feel the urge to tell them what to do? Or feel helpless around them?

Perhaps you feel sad or tearful when they bring up certain subjects? Each feeling has some meaning attached to it.

Countertransference can occur in a situation in which there is an exact parallel or only a vague connection. The only constraints are that it produces an out-of-the-ordinary feeling in the therapist. For example, if a client has lost their husband to a car crash, it would not be a stretch for the counselor to have a reaction if they, too, had lost a spouse suddenly. That connection is pretty clear.

It is also possible for the countertransference experience to be linked much more loosely, such as if a client's problems with a group of moms at her kid's school reminded the counselor about a former teacher the counselor had that embarrassed him in front of the class. The only connection there is the school, but it doesn't matter. Countertransference happens when an emotion is triggered, not necessarily when an experience is the same.

Now, I'm hoping you took my advice and dealt with what personal problems that you could before becoming a therapist. Things will come up no matter how well adjusted you are, but it is best get the work you can do out of the way beforehand! Outside of getting therapy yourself in the truly serious situations, the first step to dealing with the fairly common experience of countertransference is to separate your issue from their issue. This is necessary so that you don't allow your issues to taint your ability to help the client. Remember, the session is not about you. Shelve it for the duration of your time with your client, and deal with it when you're on your own.

When you have had some time to process, try to look at what this thing is all about. Try to find the root if at all possible. Then you have to decide what to do about it. If at any time it will compromise your client's care, the only ethical thing to do would be to refer. We work through our issues on our own time. We do not allow them to affect our clients.

Wondering how you will know if you're experiencing this or not? Any strong emotional reaction should serve as a clue to something about that person that you must monitor. Some clients you may find yourself instantly liking. It may seem cynical, but you need to examine that. It's okay to like your clients, but why do you like them? Do you find them to be intelligent, capable, or have a genuine personality? Those are among several good reasons to like your clients. But if you like your client for another reason, such as that they are very flattering about your abilities as a counselor, or ask about your life a lot, that is something you may need to examine.

It feels good to be complimented on our work! Lord knows, it's hard to come by in this field. You don't receive "progress reports" and usually the only verification that you're a good counselor is when clients refer friends and family to you. We work with language, the nuances of speech. It is not surprising that so many of us respond to verbal "pick-me-ups." And it's okay to enjoy them, for their own sake.

> *Carol's Comments:*
> Remember that dodging difficult issues with clients doesn't really help them. It's harder to confront them when you're worried about whether or not they like you.

But be careful about what they do to your counseling relationship. We respond more positively to people that seem to like us. And that may not be helpful to your client. Of course, Carl Rogers would say Unconditional Positive Regard is always a good thing, but I disagree if it keeps us from pointing out a flaw in a client's overly optimistic view of a career, relationship, or life choice. If you really like a person, it's going to be harder for you to push them when it comes to unhealthy behavior. For example, if you really like a client who came in to work on her dysfunctional relationship choices, it may be hard to address in session one day if she had, say, just slept with an old boyfriend, now a married man. "It just happened once," your client may say. "It was no big deal. We didn't plan for it, so it wasn't like we did anything wrong. It just happened."

If you really like this client, you might want to let her off the hook for that one. Allow her to brush off the significance of her decision. You must be able to retain your objectivity in order to help her grow. "Now, I hear you saying that you didn't plan for anything to happen, but you picked up the phone when he called and you let him come over to your house at one in the morning. Did you really think that wouldn't have consequences?"

To be a good counselor, you can't always be their friend. It's the same reason why you can't be your best friend's counselor. If you're the friend, your first job is to be on that person's side. If you're the counselor, the first job is to help them change in the way they want to change. They are mutually exclusive roles, and you will feel schizophrenic if you try to combine them. If my best friend is hurt or upset, I will be over there with her railing against the person who hurt her. We will eat lots of chocolate and talk about how everybody's done her wrong. Maybe a couple of days later we will talk about what she could have done to change the situation. But with a client, your first and foremost concern has to be helping them tap into the strength to take action against the problem.

It's not that you can't like them. It's just that you can never allow that feeling to cloud your judgment. Be their counselor, not their friend.

COMMON MISCONCEPTIONS ABOUT THERAPY

I am not one of those counselors who likes to talk about the horrors of television and what it's doing to our society as a whole. On the contrary, I confess I am a bit of a TV junkie. However, one thing I am *not* a fan of in the entertainment world is how they portray therapy. Carol told me she hates watching therapists on television, because, "it feels like work." I don't mind it that aspect of it, but I do mind when they show therapy in an unrealistic or unhealthy light.

I have found very few honest portrayals of how therapy works in entertainment. Most of the time, the counselors sleep with their clients (because we would really throw years of expensive education out the window for that?) or they are incredibly over-involved, coming into the client's homes, making decisions for them, and doling out medication like candy. People, this is not how therapy works.

Therapy is not about "fixing" or "saving" a person.

We are with our clients an hour a week. They are in the trenches the remaining 167 hours of the week, working out their own problems. We are a kind of consultant, trained in ferreting out mental and emotional problems and applying action to resolve those problems. Their health and sanity, though, do not depend on us, because we cannot "grant" it to them. We provide the tools, and they give it to themselves.

This is important to know first of all for the client's sake. It is so empowering for an individual, usually ashamed to be seeing a counselor, to be encouraged that they do deserve the credit for every change they make in their lives.

It's also an important realization for us. I don't know about you, but I don't want the responsibility of making someone else okay. For one thing, it's impossible. We can only do that for ourselves. For another, if I placed that burden on myself of saving others, I would constantly be falling short. I believe giving them the credit makes our treatment more effective. If we believe in them, they are more likely to believe in themselves. But if we're focusing on "fixing" their problems, we can't teach them the tools to apply themselves to other challenges in life. In reality, creating dependency would ensure that you always had a job - but at what cost?

Our job is to work our way out of a job. That idea might sound a little depressing at first, but in the years I've been in practice so far, it's really not. We don't get to save them, but we get to watch them save themselves. We get to be there. In fact, the counselor is the resource that helps them get there. That is an honor in and of itself.

<u>Therapy is not about telling someone what to do.</u>

This is another thing we often see in the movies. The therapist says, "You should do *this*." "*This* is your problem." "*I* have all the answers." Yes, in one way it can be considered that we tell clients what to do, but not really. We only provide suggestions for treatments and goals - suggestions, not advice.

People don't learn anything when it doesn't come from within. If we spend a lot of time telling people what is wrong with them and what they should do, they will stop listening to us. That is, after all, how most of the world works. Test that statement out for yourself. If you start listening for it in your sessions, you will start hearing (especially from the adolescent population) how other people have been telling them what they think the person should do all their lives. Break up with him or her. Stop doing drugs. Quit hurting yourself.

> *Carol's Comments:*
> *Telling other people what to do is easy—all the advice columnists do it—but helping clients learn to solve their own problems, that's harder and more effective in the long term.*

Whether the directives clients have been given are right are wrong, they are ineffective. Had this been a successful solution to the problem, these clients would not be in our office. Your goal is to help them find meaning and reason so that they choose healthy behaviors for themselves. It can be frustrating when you see the problem and they don't. But think of it like a secret mission. Start pointing out to them the chinks in their armor. Your goal is to get them to see for themselves *based on their own reasons* why they should or shouldn't do something.

Take, for example, teenagers, who do a lot of stupid things. I love working with them, but sorry, they do. Their brains are overrun with hormones and logic is a concept that they must be introduced to, like a stranger at a party. ("Teenager, this is logic, logic, teenager.") They must be made to see a connection between their choices and their consequences. The teenager that breaks curfew because they're having too much fun hanging out with their friends is not going to respond to parents or other adults saying "Don't ever do that again!" Why would they stop? They were having fun!

In that moment, they didn't see the potential danger, the possibilities of date rape or drunk drivers. They only saw "I was having fun and I didn't want to stop." Their perspective was limited and they didn't have the life experience yet to see what was going on from the outside.

The choice *not* to engage in these behaviors <u>must</u> be their own, or they will simply forget them again. They may still choose to forget the good choices they earlier agreed with, but their best chance at success is if the drive comes from within. Here's something you could say to a teenager to help them think through a situation: "So what happened after you broke curfew?"

Teenager: "My parents took away my phone and computer privileges, and I can't go out for two weeks."

Wise Therapist: "So because you didn't want to stop hanging out with your friends then, now you can't talk to or see your friends for two weeks."

Teenager: "Yeah."

Wise Therapist: "I guess that ended up creating a situation that was the opposite of what you wanted, huh?"

Teenager: "Oh."

You are searching for the "a-ha" moment with your client, when they connect the dots and realize for themselves what went wrong and what needs to change. The a-ha moment, not telling them what to do, is effective therapy. At that point, if you offer suggestions, they will be open to them. They will listen. *That's therapy.*

Therapy is flexible.

I am a complete Type A. You may not be, but since studies tend to show disproportionate numbers of firstborn children (who are also likely to be Type A) in higher education, it's certainly possible you understand exactly what I'm talking about! When I entered my first semester of practicum, I was sure I had things down. My theories was cognitive-behavioral and family systems, and I was all ready to plug people into my idea of how things worked.

Did you know that people don't generally behave the way you think they should?

Look, I know it was a bit naïve, but I thought if I planned everything out, nothing could go wrong. I now know that's a pretty ridiculous assumption. Before each session, I do usually have a general idea of 2-3 topics to bring up if the discussion lags, but that's it. No bigger plan. Really, there would be no point in doing so.

You never know what you're going to get when you go into work in the morning: disaster, crisis, or sometimes absolutely nothing. You can't go in with a preconceived notion of how things are going to work that day, because you will fail.

Please hear me on this one: I am not encouraging you to abandon your boundaries. Boundaries are everything in therapy. But don't place restrictions on the type of exchange you may have. If you do, you will just be frustrated. Even if you're Type A, I think you can eventually come to enjoy the unpredictability and just go with it.

Therapy is encouraging.

Sometimes I think our most important job in therapy is to believe in a person. The reason behind that, frankly, is that many times nobody else does. Isn't that sad? I am very, very fortunate, I realize, because my parents literally believe any one of their kids could do anything. Not everyone has that. Even if they did at one time, they may not now.

You can be that person for your clients. People generally want to know that they are "okay." Not that they necessarily will no longer have problems, because we can't promise that. Instead, they need to hear that there is at least the possibility of a decent person inside them. They need to know that they have intrinsic worth just by being human.

You can demonstrate the value you recognize in your clients by joining with them on their current level of functioning. It may seem difficult, based on the inevitable clash between your own values and those of your client, but you don't have to agree with them in order to join them. Even if you might never conceive of doing what they do, you can understand the feelings related to their actions. Every one of us has felt sad, or vengeful, betrayed or lonely. A person's choices of behavior may not be right, or admirable, but feelings are understandable.

As a therapist it is not our job to be the judge and jury of behaviors. We may need to point out to them how their behaviors are not productive, or costing them relationships, jobs, or friends, but we don't need to judge them. There is not a purpose in that for us. What will we add to their lives by telling them, "You're wrong?" It may be true, but we don't decide their fate. They do. Better to help them recognize the errors they have made themselves than to primly pronounce their mistakes.

Your job as a therapist is to focus on the potential of the person no matter what kind of person it is. In my degree program, the question came up whether we as counseling students believed people were basically good or basically evil. It's a worthwhile question for you to consider. Whatever your answer may be, my admonition remains the same. The most valuable thing you can do for your client is believe in them. When you stop encouraging them based on your belief in their possibility, they might as well give up on themselves too.

CHAPTER TWELVE
REFINING YOUR COUNSELING STYLE

YOUR MYERS-BRIGGS TYPOLOGY

If you haven't already taken the Myers-Briggs Type Indicator in your Testing & Assessments class, it is way beyond time to do so. Go into the pile of homework stashed in the hall closet (the one you keep meaning to go through) and pull out your score. If you did not take it in class already, go to myersbriggs.org and follow the links to find out your best option to take the test. Trust me, it's worth it.

Katharine C. Briggs and her daughter, Isabel Briggs Myers, drew on Jungian ideas of personality and years of study to develop the Myers-Briggs Type Indicator. The test has evolved into many different incarnations, but the one I will reference here is known as Step I. Personality is measured along four scales: Intraversion and Extraversion, Sensing and Intuition, Thinking and Feeling and Perceiving and Judging. Test-takers are measured along a *continuum*. This means that no one is going to have a perfect score of one personality characteristic or another. (Or at least, very rarely.) The test is designed to evaluate which characteristic is the dominant one, but actually, we all have echoes of both dichotomous traits.

> **Carol's Comments:**
> Not everyone cares about this kind of conceptual aid, but some clients feel very understood and can use this to make better choices.

It's important to note that none of these traits are so-called "bad" traits. Since I request most of my clients take the test at some point during our counseling relationship, I often find myself reassuring them that, "It's not going to diagnose you with anything!" Each personality trait has both a positive side and a negative side. As author Naomi Quenk writes in her book, *Essentials of Myers-Briggs Type Indicator Assessment*, it's about "healthy personality differences." (2009, p. 2) This assessment tool is not about condemning your own characteristics. It is about learning from the features of your personality and *making them serve you effectively.*

The MBTI can help clients understand themselves and help you, as the counselor, explain your clients' experiences to them. The concepts you will be sharing are very easy to grasp. I would urge you to research it further for yourself, starting with David Keirsey's landmark book *Please Understand Me II: Temperament, Character, Intelligence.* (1998) It's fascinating reading. His book will give you the most thorough overview of the material, so please start there if you're interested in the topic. I will not cover more than the basics of personality type in my explanation today.

For the purposes of the book you're reading now, I intend to explain how YOUR Myers-Briggs personality type can best interact with your work as a counselor. Knowing your own type gives you an indication of which areas of counseling you will be most drawn to, and which areas you may struggle with. This is a major advantage, and it will help you prevent burnout and maximize your chances of success.

Now here is the overview you were promised: The Myers-Briggs Type Indicator is composed of sixteen types within four main groups. As you may remember, each type uses a unique 4-letter combination code. The first letter will be either an E or an I, and refer to Extraverts, who gain their energy from being around other people, or Introverts, who recharge their energy from time spent alone or in introspection. The second letter will be either S, for Sensing Types, or N, for Intuitive Types. Intuitives like big ideas, concepts, and the abstract. Sensing Types (unsurprisingly) like what they can experience with their five senses. The third letter references either Feelers or Thinkers. Feelers communicate with the outside world primarily through their emotions, and are comfortable expressing their feelings in most cases. Thinking types lean more heavily on logic and objectivity. Finally, the last letter refers to either Judgers (J) or Perceivers (P). Judgers like knowing what's going to happen next, maintaining order, following schedules, and making lists. Perceivers would much rather go with the flow. They see time as fluid, and dislike boundaries or constraints. Generally, I've found them to be spontaneous and fun-loving.

This is not a thorough explanation of the characteristics, but I hope it will get you started so that you can begin taking advantage of the information immediately.

The first of the four major groups, as designated by author David Keirsey, is called the *Artisans*. These include all people with the letter type combination SP. (Sensing and Perceiving) Therapists in this group will be very experiential, work great with innovative techniques and tools, and be generous and easy-going. They will also hate the routine parts of counseling— i.e. note-keeping and required paperwork. The challenge with this group is that since they are so "in-the-moment," it can be hard for them to stay focused. And since they hate rules and schedules, it may be better for them to work with children, crisis counseling, and art therapy. (Keirsey, 1998)

Though all SPs will have the above characteristics to some level, each individual type will have their own unique strengths and weaknesses.

ESTP: The ESTP is extremely fun to be around, charismatic and always knows where the action is. The ESTP therapist will likely immediately inspire confidence with their attentiveness and gift of speech. (Keirsey, 1998) They excel at seeing options that may not be obvious to others. This is a real strength in counseling because clients can tend to have tunnel vision. However, the ESTP can easily grow bored with routine, and while great at being the "white knight" who is there in crisis, it can be difficult for them to commit to helping the person change when things get more even-keeled. This tendency usually mellows out with age, but the ESTP may do best working with children and performing persuasive roles such as child advocacy until that time.

ISTP: This generous personality has a strong protective instinct towards people they care about. They are much more gifted in action than in words; it can be hard for the ISTP to express themselves verbally. The ISTP will fare best at practical, less theory-based therapy, such as equestrian and other animal-assisted therapy. They "thrive on excitement" (Keirsey, 1998, p. 67) and so might really enjoy working at a residential treatment center or as a hospital staff counselor in which they can respond to an emergency. Like ESTPs, they're not fond of routine.

ESFP: This optimistic and kind personality loves people and is likely to be invested in other's welfare in a number of ways besides counseling. This is a sign of their good heart, but can also mean the ESFP may have trouble getting where they want to go in their therapy practice and keeping regular appointment times because so many other things occupy their time. There is a tendency in this type to avoid the discomfort of difficult and sad situations by being almost pathologically optimistic. If you are an ESFP you may need to learn to balance that tendency out. (Keirsey, 1998) Because of their spontaneous and positive nature, ESFPs are naturals in play therapy and art therapy, both of which appeal to their sense of fun.

ISFP: The ISFP is also artistically oriented. Strong feelers, they are very sensitive to other's pain and suffering. They are not especially verbal, and can appear "stand-offish," as can all introverts, but when it comes down to it these are arguably the most kind of all the types. (Keirsey, 1998, p. 73) ISFP therapists would probably do best primarily with art and music therapies, and also with psychiatric nursing, as they have a great sense of compassion.

I am sure you are seeing a theme develop as I speak of the SPs as related to alternative, non-traditional therapies. This is not to say SPs cannot capably do traditional therapy, because they can! I suggest these options because based on the way they react to the world, SPs will be happiest in an environment where they don't have to conform to a lot of rules and can experience something different every day. Whatever the mode of therapy, the SP therapist can make it more amenable to their way of doing things by allowing room for spontaneity, fun, and individuality.

The *Guardians* (SJs) maintain society, reveling in tradition and established order. They will be consistent, conscientious counselors, but might have trouble dealing with areas of gray since they see the world in black-and-white. Their best area of success is likely in the fields of case management, social work, drug and alcohol counseling, and psychiatric assistance. These are areas that will benefit from the SJs' steadiness and responsibility.

ESTJ: I am married to an ESTJ, so I am intimately acquainted with their firm sense of right and wrong, black and white, and "my way or the highway." They don't think this way out of a sense of dominance, but simply an idea that there is only one right way of doing things and they want to help you find it. It's a challenge for this type to see that there are various paths for various people. However, ESTJs are incredibly responsible and dependable. They assess and make decisions quickly and will work well with helping people in proven and practical ways. Counseling in a military or hospital setting would be ideal. Completing intakes and settings in which they can problem-solve will also likely appeal to ESTJs.

ISTJ: Like the ESTJ, the ISTJ is super-dependable. Keeping their word is the way they demonstrate a person's value to them, so they take it seriously. ISTJs are not naturally sensitive to emotions, but they care about others' well being, so the skill can be developed. They can have a tendency to be enablers in the sense that they will sometimes put the burden of other people's improvement on themselves instead of on the person truly responsible.

As with all SJs, it's a challenge for the ISTJ to step back from how they think people "should" behave and feel. ISTJs love to give in practical ways that reinforce social order, so the ISTJ might pursue social work, psychiatric work, corporate counseling, or any practice that does one established and defined kind of therapy.

ESFJ: The ESFJ brings sunshine wherever they go, and has the gift of making the person they are with feel like one of the most important people in the world. Incredible social contributors, they value other's opinions to the point they are crushed by verbal criticism. This can be challenging in the therapy arena because clients aren't focused on therapists' needs—or shouldn't be. Like the ESFP and ISFP, they are eternally optimistic and have difficulty staying in sadness very long. They are interested in many things, but always interested in people. This kind of person would make an energizing life coach or clergy counselor, and also do great as a counselor liaison to the public, speaking or writing in promotion of social causes.

ISFJ: The tenderhearted ISFJ can often appear enigmatically hard to know because their depth of caring is so intense they must shelter themselves from expressing it too much. Protective, they are often found in the military or the clergy because of their tendency to "shepherd" others to physical or emotional safety. This type can easily overwork themselves and must be vigilant about self-care. The ISFJ is also likely to be practical in their efforts to help, preferring action to too much talk. However, in certain situations, like when working with children, ISFJs can tend to over-talk young people. It is as if they believe they can thus instill in them healthy behaviors. As long as they curb that tendency, child advocacy and youth work are likely to be both appealing to and suited for the ISFJ personality.

Again, the SJ can flourish in any kind of field, but their best chance of happiness lies in working within established rules, promoting social good, and working in service to others.

The *Idealists* are the natural counselors, as their focus is on connection, seeking meaning, and the welfare of others. They have a gift for empathy and ease with emotion, but their strong ties to the emotional world can also have a downside. Idealists have difficulties maintaining boundaries and separating from painful situations. They will work best with individuals and adolescents where they can use their gift for inspiration of others.

ENFJ: The ENFJ has few rivals in their ability to influence others. Natural leaders and concerned with the individual's personal evolution, they have to be careful not to get over-involved with the person they are helping. They can see so strongly the positive possibilities in others that they can idealize their clients and risk disappointment when the person turns out to be only human, making bad choices as we all do. The ENFJ also needs to be careful they are not taken advantage of, as they are so encouraging and inspiring to be around that others can easily drain their generous resources. ENFJs make great group counselors, pastoral counselors, speakers, and professors in addition to private counselors.

INFJ: This personality makes the ideal counselor, of course – it's my personality type! While I don't know if that statement is necessarily true, the INFJ *is* known as the "Counselor" in Keirsey's book. (1998, p. 152) We INFJs are drawn to this field because we are inborn with a desire to contribute to the greater good. INFJs intuitively grasp and express emotions, and are comfortable with life's intricacies. However, we tend to be hypersensitive, over-involved perfectionists as well! The INFJ has to be careful of taking on too much responsibility for their clients, and giving themselves a break when they can't help in a tangible way. INFJs tend to fall strongly into the categories of teacher, counselor, and writer, all of which can be expressed through counselor training.

ENFP: ENFPs are great with people and capable, intuitive observers of personality characteristics. They are good at picking up on why people behave the way they do. Very empathetic, and in possession of a natural desire to help others, they are naturally persuasive and good at getting others to do what they want. If they are not careful they might get addicted to the "high" of emotional intensity and pursue that feeling beyond what is healthy, in or out of counseling practice. ENFPs tend to think if they can arrange a situation a certain way, they can almost "make" a person behave the way they think is best. They need to remind themselves that people are individual and even if they can visualize the best solution, others may not choose to follow it. ENFPs work well with adolescents and children, and may enjoy writing about emotionally charged subjects. Crisis work will likely be appealing as well, because of their love of rescuing others. If I were in crisis, I would want an ENFP on my side.

INFP: Though all four of the NFs lean towards idealism, none more than the INFP. They can picture a good thing so strongly that they can become fixated on it, unable to accept a lesser good because it is not the **ideal** good. Their intensity is characteristic of their personality: they care deeply for a few people or a specific set of causes and are very loyal. They are fairly flexible unless someone threatens an internal value, and then they cling like a bulldog to whatever issue or situation is being jeopardized. Aware of their feelings, they are good at encouraging others to express feelings. Social work, child counseling, and art therapy will be rewarding occupations for the INFP.

All NFs will feel fulfilled if their venue of therapy meets an idea of contributing and connecting meaningfully to others. NFs simply thrive on inspiring and encouraging others. If you are an NF and meet that need in your therapy practice, you will never run out of energy.

The final group, the *Rationals*, can grasp the big picture and the world of possibilities to an extent none of the other groups can touch. They are intellectually quick and great at long-term projection. However, their ability to look into the future can lead to a natural pessimism, and their high abilities translate into high standards for themselves and those close to them. Many are extremely critical of themselves, although somewhat less so of others. Rationals will likely prosper best in psychology research and "think tank" pursuits, as college professors and career counselors.

ENTJ: The ENTJ is a laser-focused leader. They have what it takes, and are happy when leading others to the right decisions. Their power of concentration and ability to summon resources towards a valued goal is unmatched. They are great communicators and can often inspire wonder in those around them. However, this population does have a hard time putting stock in feelings, whether their own or those of others around them. They simply do not see feelings as relevant in the single-minded pursuit of their goals. They may do best leading "tough love" style counseling at adolescent treatment facilities or drug rehabilitation clinics. Especially with those who have lacked structure, the leadership qualities and strong convictions of the ENTJ often inspires devotion in their clients.

INTP: INTPs have good memories and are great at seeing the world of possibilities. For every action, the INTP can tell you a thousand different directions that action can take and the results of the change. The INTP is good at seeing another person's problems and how to help them, but they <u>must</u> watch their presentation of this information, as it can come off in a critical manner, instead of a helpful one as the INTP means it to be. The INTP makes a good teacher or researcher in the psychological field. Their natural affinity towards art and music and their desire to avoid structure may also lend itself to creative therapies.

INTJ: No one can surpass the INTJ's capacity for planning and strategic thinking. Utilitarianism is the name of the game, and nothing useful goes without consideration. They dislike negativity and verbalize positive thoughts, although because of their difficulty in expressing emotions others might not always pick up on the effort. Their strict focus on the goal, like the ENTJ, can make others feel inconsequential or like they are failing when the INTJ demonstrates his or her unwillingness to compromise. INTJs are likely to be happier working with systems or procedures rather than directly with people, perhaps brainstorming creative approaches to social problems in school or public health settings. An INTJ would be excellent in psychological research or working with data. (Keirsey, 1998)

ENTP: Good with politics, outgoing, engaging and inspiring, ENTPs enjoy playing with ideas to improve function with a purpose. They are non-judgmental, curious and creative. They are inventive with everything they come into contact with, whether it is work, home life, or even conversations between friends. Routine is to be avoided at all costs and ENTPs "may create an unnecessary crisis on the job, just to give them an opportunity to come up with a solution..." (Keirsey, 1998, p. 203) Since they are quick to size up a situation and devise responses to it, they will have talent with managing large groups of people in live psychological experiments. They will probably enjoy the creative chaos of residential treatment and working with children and teenagers. Verbal fluidity and natural people skills also mean ENTPs make excellent teachers as well.

The buzzwords for NTs are "research" and "teaching." Rationals adore knowledge and thinking strategically. Though they have differing talents in doing so, they yearn to transmit their knowledge and inner world of ideas to others. As long as the NT is able to strategize and work with a great deal of input and output, they will probably enjoy their job a great deal.

YOUR AREAS OF EXPERTISE

The next step in composing an image of your personal counseling style is returning to the marketing platform developed in chapter five and really looking at your areas of expertise. You've already answered the question, "Why Counseling?" Now I want to throw another "why" at you. Why are you *good* at counseling? This is not the time to be modest. Even if you're starting out, you have personal qualities that make you a good therapist. Take the notes you (should have) started in chapter eleven about why you have chosen do this and add a section in which you can start exploring what it is about you will make others choose you to be their counselor.

Though particular skills are important, for now I would like you to focus on what qualities you have, not specifically on techniques. Start with character traits. For example: good listener, strategist, problem-solver... If you need something to help you get going, flip back to your Myers-Briggs individual personality profile. Under each type I listed several traits that are good for counselors to have. Do you identify with any of those?

> *Carol's Comments:*
> *Seeing your specific strengths is important. Our flaws will make themselves visible; talents tend to be overlooked.*

This may sound a little touchy-feely for some of you. After all, this section is entitled "Your Areas of Expertise," and you might be thinking, "Shouldn't I be talking about how well I can use the Empty-Chair Technique? Enact a psychodrama? Or ask the Miracle Question? The thing is, those *aren't* your area of expertise. They're somebody else's areas of expertise that you can mimic well. Please understand me. This is not meant to denigrate your ability in those areas at all. But I want you to focus on your own unique contributions to the field. You are *the expert* at something that only you can do.

Once you have figured out your talent, it is up to you to make a conscious decision to use that talent. I have chosen in my career to be an expert in encouragement. I like doing it, and it's fun finding the true and unique ways of building another person up. What about you?

What are you going to be an expert in? How about an expert innovator? You can provide options your clients never even knew they had. Or an expert empathizer, identifying the exact feelings a client is experiencing and putting those feelings into words for them. Possibly you will have the ability to elicit from the client only their most relevant personal history. Or maybe you'll be uniquely talented at connecting with teenagers or children. The sky's the limit!

The great part is that you don't have to stick to just one area of expertise. As you continue to grow and develop as a counselor, and you will find more springing up all the time. Once you identify some of your primary areas of expertise, your job is to find new ways to maximize their usage. Connect with the people and groups that will respond well to what you have to offer. Train in therapeutic techniques that draw upon your natural talents. And return to this list of qualities you have when you feel unmotivated and imperfect as a helper.

I *know* you can do it.

CHAPTER THIRTEEN
PREVENTING BURNOUT

B urnout in counseling: I would define this as dreading your workweek, consistently drifting off in session, picturing your clients on deserted islands far away and no longer loving your job. It happens to everyone at some point, but there's quite a bit of difference from having it come to visit and having it move in with you. For this problem, there's a quick fix, like a vacation, and a better fix: prevention.

IT CAN BE DONE

Sometimes the most difficult part to overcome when facing an obstacle is the idea that the goal is possible. We see that all the time with our clients, don't we? "I can't find a new job." "There's no men who want to date a woman after forty." If that came out in session, we wouldn't take but a minute to attack the faulty premise our client is operating with. But when it comes down to burnout, it feels as if we're not allowed to redefine terms. To hear many in the counseling profession, burnout is inevitable. It's not *if* but *when*. Therapists who have been in the profession too long without support can unfortunately be the cause of this. Experienced therapists are the only models we beginning counselors have. When they're bitter and frustrated, we see our potential future in their circumstances and cringe. There's nothing that strikes more fear in the heart of a new counselor than seeing a cranky, tired counselor rant and rave about how his or her career has been such a huge disappointment.

Hear me now: this does *not* have to be *your* destiny. I have a great friend, a counselor trainee, who shared a rather provocative statement with me. A counselor employed by a government agency told her this, "You'll find out in this job that you're nothing but other people's emotional trashcan." Excuse me, but don't you get to choose whether or not you're going to be a trashcan? It might be controversial to say, but those who hate their careers made a choice to do so. With proper education and support, avoiding burnout is possible. The danger is in internalizing the idea that you have no choice in the matter.

Burnout is not inevitable. Yes, you will have bad days. As I'm writing this, it is a long day and I'm fantasizing about being released from work to go home. It's normal to be frustrated. You may sometimes want to be in a different stage of your career than you are now. It's hard being an intern, and some places that employ counselors are just awful. Feelings like these are common - but they're not really burnout.

When I talk about burnout, I'm talking about a permanent sense of stagnancy. I believe this doesn't have to happen. I think that you get to determine your destiny for yourself. I share this with you because right now, you are in the perfect stage to adopt a revolutionary, and possibly life-altering belief: that you got into this job for success, not failure.

I think success is defined as making your job into what you want it to be, and feeling effective in your chosen field. Let's talk about some things you can do to accomplish these valuable goals.

> *Carol's Comments:*
> The term self-care has become a buzzword in our profession because you can get caught up in responding to others' needs and forget your own. Try hard not to do this. You need to care for your 'instrument'— you. Don't let money be an excuse; exercise, pursue your passions, find a hobby that you love. Take care of you.

DON'T GIVE TOO MUCH

Why do I start here? Because this is the number one compulsion I see in new counselors. We all get so excited to help people that we pour our whole selves into the job. We are riding high on the feeling of helping others.

Stop and think about it a minute. It is not helpful to others to give so much that you have nothing left for yourself. There is no quicker recipe for burnout. Feeling helpful, at first, feels great. We get all kinds of positive chemicals going off in the brain, and we think to ourselves, "Finally! Someone needs me! This is where I belong."

You set the precedent of daily emailing your client to soothe her personal crises. Now comes an evening when you have a date you've been really looking forward to and you end up missing it because a client is calling you in tears. This would be why helping too much doesn't work.

In reality, two things happen when you start out by giving too much: you implode, and your clients get worse.

"But I'm helping them," you say, indignant at my lack of empathy for your worthy goal. You are helping, in that moment. But when you give too much to your client, you create dependency. And that's not good for either of you.

> *Carol's Comments:*
> *I mean this in the nicest possible way— remember you're not God. There are other counselors, other people in clients' lives, other ways your clients will find the answers and support they need. You don't have to offer them all of you.*

If you think about it, giving less to your clients actually requires more humility than giving more to them. That might seem outrageous, but it's true. Giving less says, "I am not the be-all and end-all in this person's life. I am confident and capable of helping them, but I trust them to have the ability to take care of themselves with a balanced level of support." Giving too much sends the opposite message. "This person can't handle life without me. I must always be there for them, because I am that important to them."

Remember in earlier chapters when we've discussed the fact that you cannot save others? Yeah, I haven't forgotten that. You can save people from a burning building, but not from their emotions or life choices. They have to take on that responsibility themselves. They will develop a better self-image and sense of their own power if they do. In this way, again, you're doing what's better for them. You're leading them to good choices for their lives, but they're getting to take credit for it and learning how to repeat those good decisions under other circumstances.

If you give too much for too long, you will start hating your clients. I guarantee it. You will feel burdened by them, and in truth, you will be. Putting yourself in the position of giving more than is healthy is making yourself a servant to the job; rather than an occupation carefully and judicially managed. You've lost control, and you'll blame your clients for taking too much from you. It's much easier to circumvent this whole thing by knowing what you can handle from the beginning and giving only what you can.

SEPARATE YOUR WORK LIFE FROM HOME LIFE

Confession time. This is something I had a problem with early in my practicum. Clients would tell me their stories during the day, and I would pack them up in my laptop bag and bring them home with me. At home, I would think about the abused little girl who never got to have a childhood. Or, the schizophrenic man that never came back after the first session would flit through my mind as I was trying to calm down with a novel. I would worry about the couple I saw on the verge of divorce even as I was trying to spend quality time with my husband.

Tell me, who did that help? Not my relationship. I was engaged at the time I started practicum, and married shortly before my internship. Changing relationships have stress of their own; they didn't need the addition of my work issues as well! It didn't help the clients either. My worrying about them in off hours added nothing to my ability to work with them in session. If anything, it detracted from that, as I burned through so much energy feeling sad and concerned for them during the week, it was difficult to have energy with them in session!

My supervisor and co-author, Dr. Carol Doss, gave me advice during this time that I will never forget. She told me that as a therapist, we have to believe in the client's own power to take care of themselves. We have to believe it for them, and we have to believe it for us. Sometimes our belief, as evidenced by choosing not to worry about them in off hours, is what they need from us in order to "do life" on their own.

Sometimes it will simply be what keeps us sane.

PUT YOUR FAMILY FIRST

In order to prevent burnout it is imperative that your family be there for you. This cannot happen if they are continually providing emotional support for you and you are not capable of reciprocating for them. Though divorce can happen for a multitude of reasons, I did not want lack of attention to my personal life to result in me becoming a divorced therapist. I also didn't want to spend my life nurturing others and have kids who hated me for never being there for them. You have to learn early on the balance between working at your job and putting your family first.

> Carol's Comments:
> It is a sad reality that not all families are functional and yours may not be supportive, but you still have people in your life to whom you need to give occasional priority. You need to remember to make your needs high on your list.

How do you know the difference? Well, if it goes on *too* long, your family will be happy to tell you that you have a problem. Another indicator might be if you are listening to your own teenager talk about bullying at school and think, "ugh, is my hour up yet?" When your home life starts suffering, it's time to cut back. Don't delay. It's not worth it.

CHAPTER FOURTEEN
YOUR FUTURE AS A PROFESSIONAL COUNSELOR

The purpose of this book has been to give you practical support. But I hope that reading the preceding chapters has also inspired you. You already have so much to give, but the amazing part is that you're <u>just beginning</u>! You are well on your way, with only a few more steps to wrap up your internship experience.

TURNING IN YOUR HOURS

In order to realize all your future has to offer, you need to be officially licensed by the state. Thankfully, most state systems are set up so that the hard stuff - taking the tests, submitting most of the paperwork, and securing a site – is done up front. Once you've started down the road of accruing your hours, the only thing you *should* have to be responsible for is finishing them within the prescribed number of years. The number of hours required, as well as the length of time allowed to complete an internship, will vary. Some states also prescribe a minimum length of time an intern counselor has to complete before they are eligible to apply for licensure, in order to prevent people from fraudulently turning in their hours before they could possibly have completed them. Your record of hours will need to be signed by your supervisor. His or her signature represents both that they are verifying the quantity of hours earned and stating that he or she thinks you are competent to earn a license.

Usually when you turn in hours to the state you will simply fill in the number of hours completed, not the details of the dates and times you earned them. But I hope you've still been keeping good records for yourself, like I recommended earlier. In most cases, you won't need to make use of those records. But if you're audited, those records can save your license. So hang on to them for a while! I would suggest that you keep your detailed records 2-5 years. Determine the length of time on factors like your relationship with your supervisor (could he or she sell you out later?) and the nature of counselor licensure in your state. For example, California licensure for counselors is relatively recent, and so I would guess that California interns might be under more scrutiny for a period of time than will interns from other states.

After this, your final step in earning your license is simply mailing in the form with your licensing fee. Then you wait. It generally takes 2-4 weeks to hear back from the board, which can be agonizing. Because I do so hate to see you suffer, I'm going to let you in on a little insider secret: before you receive your license in the mail, a note of your change in status is recorded with the state board. Most state boards now have an online roster of counselors available for clients to verify counselor licensures. If you look yourself up on those rosters (provided they are a dynamic, rather than static, rosters) you can see for yourself the minute it's updated. (Dynamic rosters are updated as information changes, static rosters are published once every year or every quarter and will not be as accurate.) By checking this online roster I found out a good 7-10 days early that I was approved for my full license. Here's hoping you can too!

PROFESSIONAL MEMBERSHIPS

You can join a professional association at any time: as a student, an intern, or after you have achieved licensure, but professional membership is highly recommended at some point along the journey for the serious counseling professional.

Why? Each organization's website will spell out their particular advantages of membership, but they nearly all have certain benefits in common. One is providing a discount on various products and services necessary for professional counselors, such as liability insurance, continuing education classes, and sometimes professional education books. You're going to buy these things anyway, so why not get a good deal? Also, most professional associations also have a publication (or several) that members receive exclusive access to. The California Association of Drug and Alcohol Counselors publishes *Counselor Magazine*, while the American School Counselor Association puts out the *Professional School Counseling* journal, *ASCA School Counselor* magazine, and an e-newsletter. These publications keep you up-to-date on news and research in your field.

Each association also sponsors conferences and seminars related to their area of expertise. Members either get major discounts or are the only ones who can come to these conferences, which provide them with *priceless* opportunities to network and to learn. Networking in particular is one of the many intangible benefits people often refer to when discussing counselor organizations. It gives you a point of commonality when introducing yourself, or a means of relating to each other. There is also a level of prestige to being involved in a professional organization. It's an exclusive club, and you made it in. Professional associations don't let just *anyone* in. Membership gives new counselors credibility both to clients and to other counselors.

> **Carol's Comments:**
> This is another way you take care of yourself. Maintaining relationships with other therapists helps you be less isolated and keeps you in the loop as to what's happening in the profession.

In addition to well-known organizations like the ACA, the AAMFT, the APT, and the ASCA, serving respectively counselors, marriage and family therapists, play therapists, and school counselors, most states also have their own individual professional counseling organizations. Some counseling organizations even have associations based on U.S. districts, such as the Southwest.

If you think a professional membership is something that might be of benefit to you, I urge you to join sooner rather than later. Membership is cheapest while you're still in school, but also relatively less expensive within the first year after graduation and/or licensure. You can belong to one association or ten; it's up to you. Make your choice based on personal preference and your own professional goals.

CONTINUING EDUCATION UNITS

Did you think that once you got your license, you were done with school? Nope! Sorry, you are required to keep up with your education in the form of earning continuing education units for as long as you have your license. Fortunately, both the cost and the time investment for CEUs (also called CEs) in comparison to graduate education are greatly reduced.

CEUs can actually be pretty fun. Some CEU courses cover really specialized areas of the field that you can't focus on in a graduate program because the topic is too specific or too current to make it into the curricula. Do a little digging when completing your CEU requirements. You just might find a topic you would have wanted to learn more about anyway! CEUs can be earned online in unlimited amounts for a single low yearly fee (like at www.allceus.com, where I have contributed to some lessons) or through professional conferences, seminars, or even some books.

CEUs these days are really easy to obtain. I don't think you will have much trouble with them. However, if you are ever extremely low on cash or time, you can apply to the state board for an extension. The number of credit hours required and the type of CEUs necessary depend (as always) on the state you're earning them for. Nebraska requires 32 hours every 2 years, and 2 of those hours have to be an ethics course. North Carolina requires 40 per year. Everyone's different. You know the drill. Check with your state so that earning your CEUs can be as easy and painless as possible.

NEW OPPORTUNITIES

Possibilities are open to you as a licensed practitioner that you were barred from experiencing as a counselor intern. Now you can apply to be on insurance panels. You can apply for jobs you wouldn't have qualified for before now. You can even open your own practice, because you don't need supervision anymore.

You may decide to leap into the sea of possibilities, and if you do, congratulations and good luck to you. But it is fine if you choose to take a little time to enjoy it and adjust to your new status. It's a big change! Mostly it's exciting, but also a little intimidating too. You may need time to feel settled. If you do, that's okay. You have your entire career ahead of you. You will know when you're ready to move forward. Just tune in to your instincts, and you'll be fine.

YOUR PLANS FOR THE FUTURE

This is the most critical part of the whole book, which is why it's last. Being a counselor is not a static state. We are blessed to be in one of the most dynamic, evolving and creative fields out there. Not only as a profession, as we've just discussed, but as individuals. You do not have to do counseling tomorrow the same way you do counseling today. If it isn't working for you anymore, if your clients need a change, or if you're ready for a new challenge, you have that choice! There are literally limitless ways to explore this field.

You could start your own practice, join a group, or become a clinical director. Start a nonprofit. Visit foster children with a traveling play therapy kit. Teach. Write books. Lobby with the government for counseling-related causes. You might further develop within a subset of mainstream counseling practice: hypnotherapy, animal-assisted therapy, sand tray or more. Every day is an opportunity to follow a new inspiration.

You chose counseling and worked very hard to get where you are right now. Don't eliminate any option you might like to do, even if it's not possible for a while yet. Make a list! After jotting down everything you're interested in, keep exploring. Add new options, but also go deeper into the options you've come up with. What kind of a (fill in the blank) do you want to be? For how long? Where? When? And of course – why?

The focus of this last score competency has been on preventing burnout. The name of it is "Counselor Self-Care," but as I hope you've come to see, it's very much the same thing. If you do what you love and continue to grow in it, I don't see how you can burn out. I only see you burning brighter.

We talked in an earlier chapter about your counseling style. I would like to offer an explanation of what that is. Your counseling style is simply this: Who you are, plus what you have to offer. That's it. And that's enough. Clients don't refer their friends and family to you because you have a good education, or you wrote a certain research paper, or you wear suits to work every day. They do so because they liked your style. So get out there and show it!

Seriously, go. You're ready. I believe in you.

Have a great career!

REFERENCES:

American Counseling Association. *The ACA Code of Ethics*. Alexandria, VA, American Counseling Association, 2005.

American Psychiatric Association. *The Diagnostic and Statistical Manual of Mental Disorders*, Fourth Edition. Washington, DC, American Psychiatric Association, 1994.

Keirsey, David. *Please Understand Me II: Temperament, Character, Intelligence.* Prometheseus Books, Del Mar, CA. 1998.

Quenk, Naomi. *Essentials of Myers-Briggs Type Indicator Assessment*. Hoboken, New Jersey: John Wiley & Sons, Inc. 2009.

APPENDIX:
BEGINNING COUNSELOR RESOURCES

Professional Counseling Associations

American Counseling Association
> www.counseling.org

American Mental Health Counselors Association
> www.amhca.org

American Association of Marriage and Family Therapists
> www.aamft.org

American School Counselor Association
> www.schoolcounselor.org

The American Art Therapy Association
> www.arttherapy.org

The National Association of Social Workers
> www.naswdc.org

American Dance Therapy Association
> www.adta.org

American Music Therapy Association
> www.musictherapy.org

American Association of Pastoral Counselors
> www.aapc.org

Association for Play Therapy
> www.a4pt.org

Study Resources

National Board for Certified Counselors
> www.nbcc.org

NCE Exam Prep: Pass the National Counselor Exam® Guaranteed!
www.nceexam.com

Encyclopedia of Counseling: Master Review and Tutorial for the National Counselor Examination and State Exams. 3ʳᵈ Edition. Routledge: Howard Rosenthal, 2007.

How to Pass the National Counselor Exam...The very first time! Savvy Impressions Publishers: Julie Maurant-Brown, 2011.

Golden Test Preparation Services (NCE, CPCE) Nancy Golden www.nancygoldencounselor.com Click on *Learn More.*
Contributed by Vicki Ambrose, MA, LPC, Missouri

Practicum/Internship Resources

The Internship, Practicum and Field Placement Handbook. 6th Edition. Prentice Hall: Brian Baird, 2010.
Contributed by Laura Black, Kentucky

Private Practice Resources

Private Practice from the Inside Out
www.allthingsprivatepractice.com

Where The Client Is: Building a Better Private Practice
http://www.wheretheclientis.com/
Contributed by Lindsey Wamsley, Texas

Private Practice Online Survival Guide
>www.privatepracticeonlinesurvivalguide.com/

Influential Therapist: Your Partner in Private Practice
>www.influentialtherapist.com

Continuing Education

AllCEUs Counseling CEUs
>www.allceus.com

Technology in Counseling

Online Therapy Institute
>http://www.onlinetherapyinstituteblog.com/
>*Contributed by Lindsey Wamsley, Texas*

Treatment Resources

Therapy Worksheets
>http://therapyworksheets.blogspot.com/
>*Contributed by Lindsey Wamsley, Texas*

Clinical Handbook of Psychological Disorders, A Step-By-Step Treatment Manual. 4th Edition. The Guilford Press: David Barlow, 2007.
>*Contributed by Shellie Cheirs, Kentucky*

The *Practice Planners* series. Various authors: Wiley.

Please Understand Me II: Temperament, Character, Intelligence. Prometheus Nemesis Books: David Keirsey, 1998.

Assessment and Treatment Activities for Children, Adolescents, and Families: Practitioners Share Their Most Effective Techniques. (Vol. 1 & 2) Champion Press: Liana Lowenstein.

Contributed by Laura Black

Essentials of Myers-Briggs Type Indicator Assessment. John Wiley & Sons: Naomi Quenk.

Counselor Marketing Resources

Marketing for the Mental Health Professional: An Innovative Guide for Practitioners. Wiley: David P. Diana, 2010.

Recommended Coaches

AdvantEdge Success Coaching (Professional, Leadership, Management)

Barbara Jordan

www.advantedgesuccesscoaching.com/

Blogging With Beth (Blogging and Social Media Tips for Women)

Beth Hayden

www.bloggingwithbeth.com

David P. Diana (Marketing, Creative & Web Design, Consulting)

David P. Diana

www.davidpdiana.com

ABOUT THE AUTHORS

Stephanie Ann Adams, MA

After earning her MA in Counseling through Dallas Baptist University in 2009, Stephanie interned under Dr. Carol Doss at the Family Counseling Center in Fort Worth. She counts among her greatest professional achievements the opportunity to blog for the American Counseling Association, being named on the 2011 "Not Most People" list by author David P. Diana and of course, having the privilege of running the Beginning Counselor website.

In 2011 she relocated to College Station, TX, and started her own e-therapy business, Beginnings Counseling & Consulting, at www.stephanieadamslpc.com. In addition to her online counseling and beginning counselor coaching, Stephanie develops continuing education courses for allceus.com and provides online therapy on a contract basis for other e-counseling sites. Since May 2009 she has been married to her husband, Tim, who is currently a medical student. He doesn't always understand "all that emotional stuff" but is always supportive. This is her first book.

Carol R. Doss, PhD

Having earned a PhD in counseling, Carol works at a community agency as the Clinical Director and carries a caseload of her own clients. She is currently supervising several counselors working toward achieving licensure as Professional Counselors. She also writes a weekly advice column for the counseling center's website, www.family-counseling.org, addressing a wide variety of topics relating to human relationships.

Married since 1978 to another therapist, Carol has two adult daughters. In 2010, her book, *Should I Leave Him?* was published by Adams Media, ISBN 978-1598699692.

Carol shares this about her life: "All my significant personal endeavors—grad school, marriage, parenting and writing—have taught me that perseverance and hard work add up to success."

HUNGRY FOR MORE?

By reading this book, you've just made yourself 100% more effective as a beginning counselor. But it doesn't have to stop there. You can continue developing your counseling savvy by purchasing the companion volume to this book, ***The Beginning Counselor's Survival Guide Workbook***. It's available for instant pdf download at the Beginnings Store! Here's the address:

http://www.stephanieadamslpc.com/beginningsstore.htm

The Beginning Counselor's Survival Guide Workbook features 14 chapters of worksheets and tip sheets to make your experience as a beginning counselor easier and more successful.

Here's a sampling of what's included:

- Site Interview Questions
- Tracking Hours Worksheet
- Tips for Talking With A Difficult Supervisor
- Office Supply List
- Example Professional Disclosure Statement
- A list of Professional Liability Insurance Providers
- Boundaries Worksheet
- Client Attraction Methods Worksheet
- AND MORE!

Or, try out **Beginning Counselor Coaching!** I work with new counselors like you all the time to provide services you can't get anywhere else, like supervisor and site location, new counselor marketing, advice on starting a counseling business from scratch and applying for licensure, among many other things! I offer a moneyback guarantee and a free consultation, so contact me today at Stephanie@stephanieadamslpc.com!

CPSIA information can be obtained at www.ICGtesting.com
Printed in the USA
LVOW111329050413

327835LV00003B/11/P